Young People's Science Encyclopedia

Gr

osbeak
oundhog
oundwater
ouper
ouse

ava
uinea pig
ulf Stream
ull
appy

ymnosperm
ypsum
yroscope

Ha

aber process
abituation
afnium
ahn, Otto
ahnium
ail
air
ale, George Ellery
alf-life
alite
alley, Edmund
all-Heroult
alogen
amster
ardness scale
ardwood
arelip
arvest
arvey, William
awk
aworth, Sir Walter
awthorne
ay fever

He

eart
eart murmur
eartwood
eat
eat barrier
eat of fusion
eat of reaction

Heat of vaporization
Heavy metals
Heavy water
Heimlich's Maneuver
Helicopter
Heliograph
Helium
Hematite
Hemlock
Hemophilia
Hemp
Hench, Philip
Henry, Joseph
Hepatitis
Herb
Herbicide
Herbivore
Hercules
Heredity
Hernia
Heron
Herschel, William
Hertz
Herzberg, Gerhard
Hess, Victor

Hi

Hibernation
Hibiscus
Hiccough
Hickory
Hill, Archibald V.
Hinshelwood, Cyril
Hippocrates
Hippopotamus
Histogram
Histology
Hives

Ho

Holly
Hollyhock
Holmium
Hologram
Homeostasis
Homo sapiens
Homogeneous
Homogenization
Honeysuckle
Hoof
Hooke, Robert

Hookworm
Hop
Hormone
Horn
Horse
Horse chestnut
Horse latitudes
Horsepower
Horsetail
Horticulture
Hot springs

Hu

Huckleberry
Human being
Humidity
Hummingbird
Hurricane
Huxley, Julian S.
Huxley, Thomas H.
Huygens, Christian

Hy

Hyacinth
Hybridization
Hydra
Hydrangea
Hydrates
Hydraulic action
Hydrocarbon
Hydrochloric acid
Hydroelectric power
Hydrogen
Hydrogen bond
Hydroid colony
Hydrolysis
Hydrometer
Hydroponics
Hydroxide
Hydroxyl
Hyena
Hygiene
Hygrometer
Hypertension
Hypertrophy
Hypodermic
Hypotension
Hypothalamus

Ib

Ibex
Ibis

Ice
Iceberg

Immunity
Impetigo
Imprinting

In

Incubator
Indium
Inductance coil
Induction
Inertia
Infection
Infinity
Inflammation
Influenza
IRAS satellite
Ink
Inorganic
Insecta
Insecticides
Insectivore
Insight
Insoluble
Inspiration
Instinct
Instrument landing
Instrument panel
Insulator
Insulin
Integumentary
    system
Internal medicine
International
    Bureau of Weights
        and Measures
    Control of Natural
        Resources
    Date Line
    Geophysical Year
    Hydrological Decade
    Oceanographic
        Decade
    System of Units

YOUNG PEOPLE'S
SCIENCE ENCYCLOPEDIA

Edited by the Staff of
NATIONAL COLLEGE OF EDUCATION, Evanston, Illinois

ASSOCIATE EDITORS

HELEN J. CHALLAND, B.E., M.A., Ph.D.
  Chairman, Division of Natural Sciences
  National College of Education,
  Evanston, Illinois

DONALD A. BOYER, B.S., M.S., Ph.D.
  Science Education Consultant, Winnetka
  Public Schools, Winnetka, Illinois
  Science, National College of Education

EDITORIAL CONSULTANTS
ON THE STAFF OF NATIONAL COLLEGE OF EDUCATION

Elizabeth R. Brandt, B.A., M.Ed.
Eugene B. Cantelupe, B.A., M.F.A., Ph.D.
John H. Daugherty, B.S., M.A.
Irwin K. Feinstein, B.S., M.A., Ph.D.
Mary Gallagher, A.B., M.A., Ph.D.
Beatrice S. Garber, A.B., M.S., Ph.D.
Hal S. Galbreath, B.S. Ed., M.S.
Arthur J. Hannah, B.S., M.Ed., Ed.D.

Robert R. Kidder, A.B., M.A., Ph.D.
Jean C. Kraft, B.S., M.A., Ph.D.
Elise P. Lerman, B.A., B.F.A., M.F.A.
Mary M. Lindquist, B.A., M.A., Ph.D.
Mary-Louise Neumann, A.B., B.S.L.S.
Lavon Rasco, B.A., M.A., Ph.D.
Bruce Allen Thale, B.S.Ed., M.S.Ed.
Fred R.Wilkins, Jr., B.A., M.Ed., Ph.D.

SPECIAL SUBJECT AREA CONSULTANTS

Krafft A. Ehricke, B.A.E., H.L.D.
Benjamin M. Hair, A.B., M.D.
Charles B. Johnson, B.S., M.A., M.S.
Raymond J. Johnson, B.B.A., M.Ed.

H. Kenneth Scatliff, M.D.
Eleanor S. Segal, M.D.
Paul P. Sipiera, B.A., M.S.
Ray C. Soliday, B.A., B.S., M.A. (Deceased)

Don Dwiggins, Aviation Editor

THE STAFF

Project Director   Rudolph A. Hastedt
Project Editor   M. Frances Dyra
Editorial Assistant   Janet Zelasko

Young People's
SCIENCE
Encyclopedia

Edited by the Staff of
NATIONAL COLLEGE OF EDUCATION
Evanston, Illinois

Volume 9/Gr-In

 CHILDRENS PRESS, CHICAGO

Photographs

Page 2:   Skylab space station (NASA)

Page 3:   *Top to Bottom:*
          Wheatfield (U.S.D.A. Photo)
          Technician capping Abbokinase (Abbott Laboratories)
          Spider (Macmillan Science Company)
          View of Earth (NASA)
          Space Shuttle (NASA)
          Bahama coral reef (Macmillan Science Company)

Cover: Design by Sandra Gelak
          Sparrow hawk (Tom Smylie: U.S. Fish & Wildlife Service)
          Silver Eagle Helicopters (U.S. Army Photo)
          Horses (James P. Rowan)

          Library of Congress Catalog Card Number: 67-17925

Copyright © 1982, 1978, 1970 by
Regensteiner Publishing Enterprises, Inc.
Copyright © 1963 by Childrens Press, Inc.
All rights reserved. Printed in the U.S.A.
Published simultaneously in Canada.

4 5 6 7 8 9 10 11 12 R 85 84 83 82

The grosbeak, a songbird, and the ground hog, a burrowing rodent, are common in America

Grosbeak (GROHS-beek) These are seed-eating birds with short, thick bills for cracking seeds. One of the best known is the crested bright red CARDINAL.

In the east the blue grosbeaks are found in the northern United States. West to Kansas are rose-breasted varieties. The grosbeaks are brightly colored like the BUNTINGS but are much larger birds. Both birds, however, are in the same family.

Aside from seeds, grosbeaks eat quantities of berries, leaf and flower buds, and insects. Many of the insects the grosbeaks eat are crop pests.

Eggs are usually a light blue, sometimes with brown spots. The rose-breasted males help incubate the eggs, but cardinals and the blue grosbeaks confine themselves to helping feed the young nestlings. After the mating season is over, most male grosbeaks lose their colored plumage and resemble the dull-colored females. The grosbeaks are all song-birds.   J. C. K.

SEE ALSO: FINCH, SPARROW

Ground effect machines see Air-cushion vehicles

Ground (electric) Those points in an electric circuit at the *zero reference value,* or voltage measurements, are said to be at *ground potential.*

Groundhog Another name for this MAMMAL is *woodchuck.* It belongs in the squirrel family. It has a large, stocky body with a blunt nose and a short, not very bushy, tail. Ears are small and rounded at the top. The hair is frosty brown and coarse. Both sexes look alike.

On the front feet are four toes and a small useless thumb. Hind feet have five toes.

Groundhogs hibernate in the winter from October to February. Legend has it that if they see their shadows when they emerge, they return to hibernation, and there will be six more weeks of winter. This is not true, but they may hibernate until green plants sprout.

They live in underground burrows. These are often on slopes where the drainage is better. Two to six young are born in spring. Eyes open at 4 weeks, and groundhogs are mature by fall.   J.C.K.

SEE ALSO: HIBERNATION, RODENTIA

Groundwater Groundwater is that water found in the upper part of the Earth's crust. It is derived almost entirely from rain. The upper level of groundwater is called the WATER TABLE.

SEE ALSO: RIVER, WATER CYCLE

Yellowfin grouper can change color rapidly

Grouper These fish, found primarily in the West Indies, weigh from 5 to 50 pounds (2.27 to 22.68 kilograms) and are in the BASS family. They blend with backgrounds by rapidly changing color.

Grouse These are popular game birds related to the domestic chicken. Nostrils and legs are feathered, and their short bills curve down. Body feathers are gray-brown with barred or striped markings. Tails are fan-shaped or pointed.

Many grouse have a bare red spot above the eye. They are ground birds, walking more often than flying. Some have feathered or horny ridges on their toes to help them walk on snow. For winter cover they need forest. In spring and summer they prefer open grassland with some brush for nesting. Females lay 9 to 12 tan eggs which incubate in about 3½ weeks. Young begin to fly when twelve days old. J. C. K.

The prairie chicken is a kind of grouse

Guava The shrub or small tree bearing this FRUIT grows to 30 feet (9.14 meters) high. The yellow berry is round or pear-shaped. The white, yellow, or pink pulp has many seeds.

Simple, opposite LEAVES are evergreen. The white, perfect FLOWER has five petals and many stamens. It is about 1 inch (2.5 centimeters) across. The fruit is high in vitamins A, B, and C (ascorbic acid). Strawberry guava has white flowers also, but smaller fruit. Red exocarp or skin surrounds the white pulp.

Guava belongs to the Myrtaceae family. It is propagated by seeds or budding. H.J.C.

SEE ALSO: PLANTS, TROPICAL

Guavas grow in tropical areas

Guided missile see Bomb, Missile

Guinea hen see Fowl

Guinea pig The domestic guinea pig is not related to pigs but is a *cavy*. Cavies are South American RODENTS. The first cavies were brought to Europe from Dutch Guiana, which later became Guinea. The name *pig* came from the fact that these animals make a piglike grunt when they are hungry.

Guinea pigs are usually small with fat bodies, short legs, and no tails. Their ears are small and rounded at the tips. The wild ones have red or gray-brown coats. Domestic ones come in many colors but spotted is usual.

In nature, they live in underground burrows. They like areas with lots of brush rather than open prairies. They feed on all types of vegetation which gives them water.

Guinea pigs, whether domestic or wild, are very fertile animals. Wild types will bear two or three young in a litter and will produce two litters a year. The domesticated ones have

A guinea pig

three or four in a litter and produce five or six litters each year.

Gestation, or the time between the union of egg and sperm (*fertilization*) and birth, takes about two months. The young are well-developed at birth. They are able to feed themselves when only a day old. When two months old they are capable of reproducing.

In spite of the fact that female guinea pigs have several young to feed in each litter, they have only two *teats,* or nipples. Milk produced by the mammary glands of all mammals always contains about the same ingredients but the proportions of these vary with the species of mammal. Milk contains water, butterfat, milk sugar (*lactose*), albumin, and various salts. If the albumin content is high, the rate of growth is increased. Guinea pigs' milk is very high in albumin so that young guinea pigs double their weight in just a few days. In contrast, human milk is low in albumin so that the human infant takes about three months to double its birth weight.

Domesticated guinea pigs are used in experimental laboratories. They are small, will eat commercial rabbit food, produce several litters a year, are not susceptible to many diseases and live about eight years. However, they cannot withstand sudden changes in temperature and tend to have an unpleasant odor. In South America they are a source of meat. J. C. K.

Gulf A gulf is a large body of water surrounded on three sides by land. A BAY is similar to a gulf but is much smaller. The Gulf of Mexico, which lies to the south of the central United States, is a well-known gulf. It greatly affects the weather of the United States.

Gulf Stream One of the best-known ocean currents is the Gulf Stream. This "river" in the ocean moves tons of water every second. The Gulf Stream is an extension of the North Equatorial Current. The current is moved by steady and strong easterly winds through the area of Cuba and the Central American coast. It piles up in the Gulf of Mexico to such an extent that sea level there is actually higher than it is in the Atlantic. This mass of water

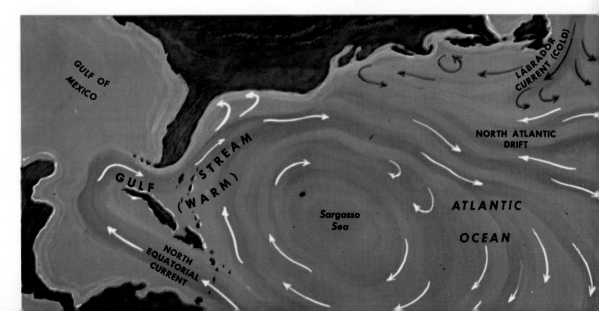

passes the tip of Florida and enters the Atlantic as the Gulf Stream.

As the Gulf Stream enters the Atlantic, it turns northward and flows past the southeast coast of the United States. Its average width is about 50 miles (80.47 kilometers); its average depth, 1,500 feet (457.2 meters). Its velocity, at times, will be as high as 5 miles (8.05 kilometers) per hour. It carries millions of tons of water, a flow that is more than a thousand times greater than the Mississippi River.

As the Gulf Stream continues to flow northward past New England, it meets the cold *Labrador Current*. Since the Gulf Stream is composed of warm, tropical waters, the meeting of a warm current and a cold current brings about great layers of fog in the area of the GRAND BANKS. At this point the Gulf Stream is slowed down and it splits into two minor branches and one main branch. A northern branch moves toward the west coast of Greenland while the other minor branch flows past the southwest coast of Iceland. The main branch continues to flow eastward. This extension is known as the *North Atlantic Drift*.

The Gulf Stream acts as an important climatic control for areas along the eastern coast of the United States and for much of northern Europe. Along the east coast of the United States, it often causes the climate to be quite cold, even though it is a warm current. This happens because the air over the Gulf Stream is warmed, creating low pressure. Cold, dry, high-pressure air far inland moves to the east to replace the warm, rising air over the ocean, bringing cold weather to the coastal regions. Much of northern Europe is warmer than one would expect for the latitude. The warm North Atlantic Drift warms the *prevailing westerlies* which, in turn, have a modifying effect on much of Europe's climate.

Benjamin Franklin was one of the first to become aware of the presence of the Gulf Stream. He noted that mail ships from England took two weeks longer in coming from England than on their return trip. He talked to many whaling captains about this to gather further information and in 1779 drew and published the first chart of the Gulf Stream.   H. S. G.

SEE ALSO: CURRENTS, OCEAN; GRAND BANKS; OCEANOGRAPHY

F. A. Blashfield

Gulls swarm over fishing boats

Gull These are large swimming birds living along the Atlantic coast. A few live around fresh water. Many gulls are gray with black and white markings. Others are all white.

Feet and bills are often brightly colored. Gulls are web-footed like ducks and their fourth toe is very small or missing.

Gulls are surface feeders and scavengers. They live on refuse and dying water life which surfaces, often near harbors. In cleaning up the harbors, they perform a service for man.

Gulls are often confused with the smaller *tern*. Gulls have squared-off rather than forked tails, shorter bills with a hook at the end, and wider wings. When picking food from the surface of the water, gulls do not dive and plunge as do terns. Both birds belong to the family Laridae.   J. C. K.

Gum (anatomical) see Teeth

Gum (botanical) A gum is a thick, sticky, complex CARBOHYDRATE which either dissolves or swells in water. Gums are usually plant or tree products or marine plant and seed extracts. Their physical properties make them useful.

Gum Arabic Gum Arabic comes from the *acacia* tree of arid North Africa. It is used in the manufacture of AD-HESIVES, textiles, leathers, polishes, water paints, food products, inks and ceramics.

Gun A gun is a WEAPON which is used to fire bullets or shot. The projectiles are forced from a long metal tube by the pressure of gas from fired EXPLOSIVES.

Gunpowder Gunpowder is an explosive mixture made of the elements sulfur, carbon, nitrogen, potassium, and oxygen. The sulfur is the native yellow solid, and the carbon is generally added as charcoal. The nitrogen, potassium, and oxygen are supplied in the form of the compound potassium nitrate.

For centuries this mixture, made in various proportions, was the only effective explosive. It was widely used for propelling the missile in GUNS of many different bore diameters. It was also used to demolish fortifications, and to loosen minerals and rock deposits in mining and construction.

Its invention is credited to the Chinese, but it was introduced into the Western world by Berthold Schwartz, a German alchemist, and Roger Bacon, an English monk, in the thirteenth century. Before gunpowder was introduced, the bow and arrow was the principal weapon used by individual soldiers.

Modern nitro-type explosives have replaced gunpowder in all but display fireworks. Present-day gun cartridges employ nitrocellulose propellants. Nitroglycerine, in the form of DYNAMITE, is in common use as an industrial explosive.

No amateur chemist should *ever* attempt to make gunpowder in home or school laboratory, for the chance of his becoming maimed or killed is great indeed. Research indicates that 90 percent or more of all student laboratory accidents occur while making such explosives. C. F. R.
SEE ALSO: EXPLOSIVES, NITROGLYCERIN, WEAPONS

✳ **THINGS TO DO**

RAISING GUPPIES

1 Prepare an aquarium allowing at least a quart (.95 liter) of hot water for every pair of guppies.

2 Supply ample plant life to provide adequate hiding places for the young. The mother guppy eats many things, including her offspring.

3 Do not let the temperature fall below 70° F. (21.1° C.) or rise above 100° F. (37.8° C.). Guppies thrive in warm waters.

4 Guppies are live-bearers. When the female guppy is about to produce young, or is "gravid," place it in another aquarium immediately.

5 Feed guppies commercial fish food, only a small pinch every other day.

Guppy These are tiny freshwater fish about 2½ inches (6.35 centimeters) long. They live well in tanks, rapidly producing large numbers of young. Guppies reproduce so often that they have been nicknamed "million fish."

Males are brilliantly colored with black spots. Color and pattern vary because of differences in control by *hereditary* factors and HORMONES.

Fins do not bear spines. In Nature the tail is moderately long, that of the male being longer. Breeders of aquarium guppies have developed a variety of tail lengths and forms.

Guppy is the popular name for one species, *Lebistees reticulatus,* of a large family of live-bearing minnows, Poeciliidae. They are entirely New World forms. Most of the family live in South America with a few in the southern United States.

Males fertilize the females internally with a long modified anal fin. One fertilization lasts for several broods. The female carries its fertile eggs in the ovary. Young are born through the *genital pore.* The female does not feed the embryos. They feed upon yolk in the eggs. Mammals are VIVIPAROUS because the embryos are fed and protected by the mother. The guppy provides protection only. Their reproduction is *ovoviviparous.* J. C. K.
SEE ALSO: AQUARIUM, TROPICAL FISH

MALE CONE

FEMALE CONE

CYCAD

GINKGO

PONDEROSA PINE

HEMLOCK

Chicago Natural History Museum

Some modern gymnosperms and the giant gymnosperms of the Carboniferous Age (inset)

Gymnosperm (JIM-no-sperm) Gymnosperms are plants which bear unprotected or naked seeds, usually in cones. Most are *evergreen* and have hard, narrow, needle-shaped LEAVES. There are about eight hundred species of the gymnosperms, including the PINE, spruce, sequoia, and GINKGO trees. Most living gymnosperms are trees, but a few are shrubs.

About 240 million years ago, during the Carboniferous period, the gymnosperms were the common variety of plant. Dinosaurs roamed under these giant trees which covered the earth. When these plants died, their bodies, pressed in the earth, formed the COAL which is mined today. Three of the seven groups of gymnosperms which lived then are extinct today. However, some palm-like *cycads* in the tropics, and the ginkgo or maidenhair tree, common in the Orient, are only slightly changed descendants of gymnosperms living then. Gymnosperms today are found throughout the world. Some types live in the tropics and subtropics, others in the desert, still others in cold northern areas. This last group includes the oldest and largest living thing, the SEQUOIA tree. This

giant tree grows to 300 feet (91.44 meters) tall and weighs about 12 million pounds (5.4 million kilograms). Another of this group, the REDWOODS of the Pacific Coast, though more than 4000 years old, are still growing.

The sequoia belongs to a group of gymnosperms called *conifers*. The spruce, pine, fir, yew, cypress, cedar, and tamarack are also conifers or cone-bearing plants. Cones are either male (pollen-producing), or female (seed-producing). The male cone is bumpy, but lacks the wooden scales of the female cone. The egg or ovule is located under the scale of the cone. No gymnosperm ovules are covered by an ovary as flowering plant (ANGIOSPERM) ovules are. The POLLEN grain forms a tube which grows into the ovule, and the second year, the naked seed, without fruit or husk around it, is produced.

Conifers are the most useful plants in existence except for food plants. They provide soft wood lumber and are grown for profit on sandy and rocky soil or in swampy land where no other crop could be grown. They are used to produce paper, pitch, turpentine, oils, and varnish. Some varieties are grown for ornamental purposes.

The next most common group of gymnosperms is the CYCADS or palm ferns. Today these grow only in the tropics. The seeds of the cycads are brilliant scarlet, yellow, or orange. Seeds are grown either on the edge of the leaf or, more commonly, in cones. Cycads range in height from a few feet or meters to 50 feet (15.24 meters). They live about 100 years. Varieties of cycads are seen today as ornamental trees in Japanese gardens. Cycads were once common in the United States, and a large fossil forest exists today in the Black Hills at Cycad National Monument. FOSSIL cycads apparently lived for about one thousand years. They produced one huge cone at the end of this time and then died.

The third group of gymnosperms has only one living member, the ginkgo tree. The ginkgo sheds its flat, fan-shaped leaves each autumn. In spring, male trees form yellow, pollen-producing *catkins.* Female trees produce a shoot with a pistil at the end which contains an ovule. When fertilized, the ovule develops into a seed with a fleshy yellow coat. This coat has an unpleasant smell because of butyric acid. Male ginkgo trees are more frequently cultivated. Ginkgo trees grow in any good soil and are little affected by city smoke. Ginkgo trees are native to China but are cultivated throughout the United States.

The fourth and last living group of gymnosperms is the *Gnetales.* They are tropical and subtropical low-growing shrubs and have a few fossil forms.   J.K.L.

SEE ALSO: PLANTS, CLASSIFICATION OF

Gypsum (JIPP-sum) Gypsum is a mineral made up of a compound of calcium, sulfur, oxygen, and water. It is usually white to yellow in color although it is sometimes found in a variety of colors. It is used in making plaster.

The chemical formula of gypsum is $CaSO_4 \cdot 2H_2O$. It has a hardness of 2 and its specific gravity ranges from 2.2 to 2.4. Gypsum is found to occur in many varieties. One of the most common forms is that of *selenite,* which has transparent to translucent crystals and is colorless. The principal use of gypsum is as a source of plaster of paris (named for the large deposits that are found in the Paris Basin). To make it, gypsum is heated to drive off most of the water that it contains. Gypsum is often found near *halite* (salt) deposits. H. S. G.

Gyroplane see Autogiro

Gyroscope (JYE-ruh-scope) A gyroscope is a device that keeps its position due to a spinning part called a *rotor.* The axle or axis of the wheel type apparatus points in a particular direction unless forces act on the spinning body.

All spinning objects, whether planets, atoms, wheels, or tops, behave in similar ways when a force attempts to change the position of their spinning axis. The object does not move as it is pushed, but instead twists with a motion about another axis which is at right angles to the spinning axis as well as at right angles to the axis of the applied force.

When held in a set of gimbals, the stable position of a gyroscope can be used as a gyrocompass to aid in navigation. A large spinning gyroscope positioned in a ship prevents "roll," or a smaller system of gyroscopes control fins that act to prevent "rolling."

A bullet is given a spin axis by the rifling in a gun barrel which keeps it aimed at the target.

MISSILES and SATELLITES use gyroscopic mechanisms to adjust and guide their position. In the case of a photographic satellite which must continually point its lens at the earth, the effects of gravitation upon gyros operate small motors which turn "against" a gyroscope in the satellite, causing the position of the satellite to change.   F. R. W.

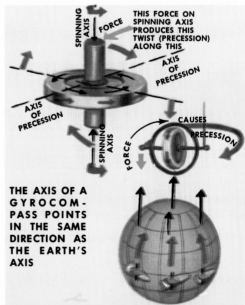

THIS FORCE ON SPINNING AXIS PRODUCES THIS TWIST (PRECESSION) ALONG THIS AXIS OF PRECESSION

SPINNING AXIS

FORCE

AXIS OF PRECESSION

CAUSES PRECESSION

THE AXIS OF A GYROCOMPASS POINTS IN THE SAME DIRECTION AS THE EARTH'S AXIS

Haber process The Haber process is used for making AMMONIA from the pure elements of hydrogen and nitrogen. It was named for a German chemist, Fritz Haber, who was able to make this process work for the first time in 1913.

Before Haber's time, it was known that an electric spark could make ammonia from the elements, but the amount produced was very small. Since the reaction gave off heat, Haber discovered that the actual heating of a mixture of hydrogen and nitrogen could give a higher yield of ammonia, if the pressure were also increased. In addition to observing the temperature and pressure requirements, Haber also used a CATALYST, which is a substance that tends to speed up a reaction without actually taking part in the reaction. In the special case of the Haber process, metals such as OSMIUM and various activated iron catalysts have been used. Since osmium is very expensive, iron powder with added potassium and aluminum oxides are used today.

In Haber's time, the temperature used was about 600° C. (1112° F.) and the pressure was 2940 pounds per square inch (152,000 mm of mercury or 200 atmospheres). These conditions gave a yield of about 8 to 13 per cent ammonia. Today's yield is 40% to 42%. The increase in amount of ammonia is due to the use of higher pressures and improved catalysts. Pressures equal to 1000 times normal atmospheric pressure are not unusual in today's Haber-type process.

In the Haber process there are actually forces working against each other. Although an increase in temperature usually increases the yield of a product in a chemical reaction, because it speeds up the reaction, this is not true in the Haber process. It is for this reason that high pressures and a good catalyst must be used in order to overcome the relatively low temperatures that must be maintained. M.S.

Habitat A habitat is the place where a certain animal or plant would naturally live or grow. For example, a warm, damp region is the habitat of FERNS, an OCEAN is the habitat of whales, and a burrow is the habitat of rabbits.

SEE: BALANCE OF NATURE, ECOLOGY, ECOSYSTEM

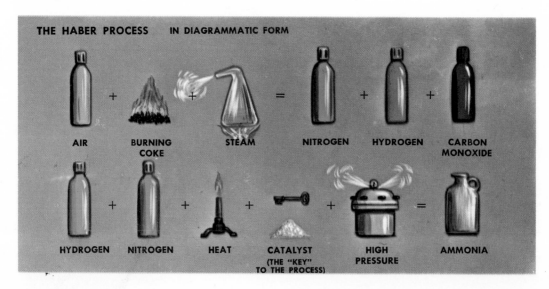

THE HABER PROCESS IN DIAGRAMMATIC FORM

AIR + BURNING COKE + STEAM = NITROGEN + HYDROGEN + CARBON MONOXIDE

HYDROGEN + NITROGEN + HEAT + CATALYST (THE "KEY" TO THE PROCESS) + HIGH PRESSURE = AMMONIA

Habituation (hab-ITCH-u-a-shun) Habituation is a simple type of learning. When an animal receives an unimportant *stimulus* again and again it will soon ignore it. A cat jumps at a loud noise. If the noise is repeated several times, the cat will not respond if no reward or punishment is involved in the disturbance.

Haddock is a common food fish

Haddock These fish are related to the cod. They are bottom feeders eating small mollusks, crustaceans, and worms. They are silvery or golden with three dorsal and two anal FINS. Pelvic fins are in front of the pectorals. It is an important food FISH.

Hafnium (HAFF-nee-um) Hafnium, element number 72, Hf, was discovered by Georg von Hevesy and D. Coster in 1923. Hafnium is the Latin name for Copenhagen.

Hafnium is considered to be a rare metal, but it is more common than lead. It has an atomic weight of 178.49.

In order to obtain pure Hf, special purification methods must be used. One of the important methods makes use of an ION exchanger. An example of an ion exchanger is the household water softener.   J. R. S.
SEE ALSO: ELEMENTS

Hahn, Otto (1879-1968) Otto Hahn is the German physical chemist who, with Fritz Strassmann, first split the URANIUM atom by bombarding it with neutrons. Born in Frankfort am Main, Hahn studied at the universities of Marburg and Munich. From 1928 to 1944 he was director of the Kaiser Wilhelm Institute for Chemistry in Berlin-Dahlem. In 1917 Otto Hahn and Lise Meitner, leading professor of the Kaiser Wilhelm Institute, discovered the radioactive element PROTACTINIUM.

Lise Meitner (1878-1968), Viennese-born physicist, professor and mathematician, is widely recognized for her work on the products of disintegration of radium, thorium, and actinium; on the behavior of beta rays; and on the nucleus of the atom. In 1939 she and Otto Frisch announced their mathematical interpretation of the work done by Hahn and Strassmann the year before they split the uranium atom with neutrons.

Meitner and Frisch also revealed mathematically the reason for the presence of barium, which Hahn and Strassman had identified as being produced by the neutron bombardment, as well as the reason for the great energy released from splitting the atom. Lise Meitner's work prepared the way for the discovery of chain reaction and the development of the atomic bomb.

Otto Hahn feared that his discovery of splitting the uranium atom would be used for the production of weapons of war. He hoped it would not. Ardently desiring peace, Hahn joined seventeen other scientists in April of 1957 to declare that they would not in any way cooperate in the building of atomic weapons. They also supported Albert Schweitzer's plea for discontinuation of atomic bomb tests.   D. H. J.

Hahnium (HAY-knee-um) Hahnium, element 105, was first reported by a group of Soviet scientists headed by G.W. Fierov in 1967. Hahnium was first produced by bombarding americium-243 with neon-22. The element is named for Otto Hahn.

In 1970 hahnium was prepared by an American team at the University of California at Berkeley. The Americans bombarded californium-249 with nitrogen-14. The product of the reaction was hahnium-260. It had a half-life of 1.6 seconds. Hahnium has been produced in a heavy ion linear accelerator by a team led by Albert Ghiorso. They bombarded berkelium-249 with oxygen-16. The isotope formed decayed by alpha decay to lawrencium-257. Its half-life is 1.8 seconds. The longest lived isotope of hahnium is hahnium-262 with a half-life of 40 seconds.   A.J.H.

Charles B. Johnson

Hailstones compared to a golf ball

Hail Hail is a frozen raindrop on which additional layers of water often collect and freeze. Hail may be the size of a large raindrop to larger than a baseball. Hail is most often formed in summer THUNDERSTORMS.

Hail is associated almost exclusively with *cumulonimbus* thunderstorms. This type of storm has very violent vertical currents within it. As condensation takes place and forms the cumulonimbus clouds, precipitation starts to fall as rain. Some of the raindrops are caught up by rising vertical currents and carried up to areas that are below freezing. The raindrop is then frozen and starts to fall. As it falls through the clouds it picks up more moisture. Then it is carried up again, and another layer forms.   H. S. G.

SEE ALSO: PRECIPITATION, WEATHER

Cross-section of hair in the scalp

©Denoyer-Geppert Co.

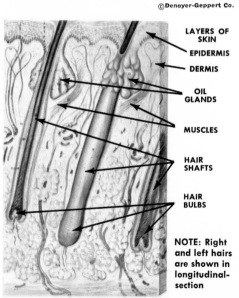

LAYERS OF SKIN

EPIDERMIS

DERMIS

OIL GLANDS

MUSCLES

HAIR SHAFTS

HAIR BULBS

NOTE: Right and left hairs are shown in longitudinal-section

Hair Hair is a protector of the body. Every hair grows from a special place in the SKIN. There are six layers to a single hair all coming from one hair-bulb. OIL GLANDS, usually two to each hair, keep the hair from becoming dry and cracking. Some animals have muscles attached to each hair which allow them to move. There are no nerves in the hair so no pain is felt when it is cut. One of the characteristics of mammals is that they have hair.

The difference between curly and straight hair is in the shape of its cross-section—round or circular in straight hair, flattened or oval in curly hair.

The cells of hair have PIGMENT giving it its color. As man grows older the ability to make pigment ceases and hair turns gray. This graying occurs in animals, also.

Hair of animals is very important. It is carefully removed from the hide and is used in hair mattresses, upholstered furniture, and felt. Fine hair from the inside of a camel's ear is used in artists' paint brushes. Pigs' hair is used for hairbrushes. Other hairs are used as binder with plaster and mortar in a house. Some kinds of fertilizer have coarse hair in them.   B. J. C.

SEE ALSO: MAMMALIA

Hair follicle see Skin

Hale, George Ellery (1868-1938) George Hale was a United States astronomer. He made important studies of the sun, stars, and planets. He helped to design and build many great TELESCOPES, which are still used.

Hale was an astronomer and an *astrophysicist*. He was a pioneer in the technology and use of telescopes.

He was instrumental in building the 40-inch (102-centimeter) reflecting telescope at the Yerkes Observatory. Still in use today, it is the largest of its kind. He also developed the 200-inch (508-centimeter) Palomar telescope. Hale is also known for perfecting the *spectral heliograph*. His original research in solar and stellar astrophysics led to the discovery of magnetic fields in sun spots.

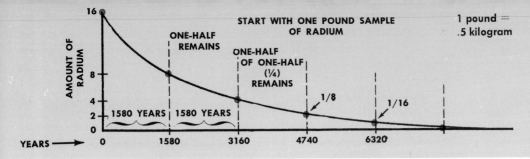

ONE-HALF
REMAINS

ONE-HALF
OF ONE-HALF
(¼)
REMAINS

START WITH ONE POUND SAMPLE
OF RADIUM

1 pound =
.5 kilogram

1/8

1/16

AMOUNT OF RADIUM

16

8

4

2

0

1580 YEARS | 1580 YEARS

YEARS ➝

0   1580   3160   4740   6320

Hale helped establish the Kentwood Observatory in Chicago, the Mt. Wilson Observatory in California, and the California Institute of Technology. He also directed the Yerkes Observatory in Wisconsin. A.J.H.

Half-life The half-life of a radioactive element is the time that it takes for one-half the atoms of the element to change into another element by automatic decay. Elements have particles called *protons* and *neutrons* which make up the center part or nucleus of each atom of the material. Protons and neutrons are not in balance in a radioactive substance as they are in stable elements such as natural iron or copper. The extra particles will tend to leave the atom.

ISOTOPES of elements which are radioactive have extra neutrons which were acquired in the original formation of the element, or perhaps acquired when the element was bombarded by nuclear particles.

Every radioactive isotope breaks down at its own rate. The surplus particles leave and a new kind of atom forms. It takes a certain amount of time for *half* of the atoms to do so, then the same amount of time for half the remaining atoms, and so on.

An example is radium. It changes into different, lighter, radioactive elements which in turn lose more particles in further breakdowns until it becomes lead. Lead is stable.

The half-life of radium is 1580 years. One-half of the atoms in a sample of radium will be changed by then. 1580 more years will lapse before one-half of the remaining atoms change.

Elements with short half-lives radiate more strongly than those with long half-lives. Radium is 2000 times more radioactive than uranium which has a half-life of over 4 billion years. Some elements have half-lives of only minutes or seconds. F. R. W.

SEE ALSO: ELEMENTS, RADIATION

Halibut see Flounder

Halite Halite, NaCl (sodium chloride), is the mineral name for common table salt. It occurs in large deposits that were formed by the evaporation of seawater. It is used to flavor food.

Halite crystallizes in the shape of a cube, and has prominent three-directional cubic cleavage. Although it can be a variety of colors, it is normally gray because of small amounts of clay in it. It is a soft mineral and is often very brittle and transparent. Halite is found throughout the world, with large deposits found in Siberia (USSR), Ontario, Michigan, and Kansas. P.P.S.

Halley, Edmund (1656-1742) Edmund Halley was an English astronomer whose name was given to a COMET which is seen every seventy-five years. Through the use of a telescope, Halley was the first person to catalog accurately the stars in the Southern Hemisphere.

Born in London, Halley was educated at St. Paul's School, London, and Queen's College, Oxford. After graduating he traveled to the island of Saint Helena, where Napoleon was later exiled, to catalog the stars in the Southern Hemisphere. Then from 1698 to 1702 he studied the orbits of the comets as he traveled throughout the Atlantic Ocean and along the English Channel on the first sea voyage ever undertaken for purely scientific purposes. As a result, his great work, *A Synopsis of the Astronomy of Comets,* was published.

Upon his return, Halley became a professor of GEOMETRY at Oxford. Later he was named Astronomer Royal at the Greenwich Observatory. He remained at this post, studying comets and the movement of the moon, until his death. D.H.J.

SEE ALSO: ASTRONOMY

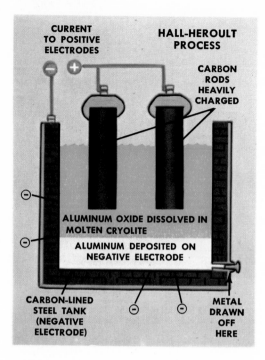

CURRENT TO POSITIVE ELECTRODES

HALL-HEROULT PROCESS

CARBON RODS HEAVILY CHARGED

ALUMINUM OXIDE DISSOLVED IN MOLTEN CRYOLITE

ALUMINUM DEPOSITED ON NEGATIVE ELECTRODE

CARBON-LINED STEEL TANK (NEGATIVE ELECTRODE)

METAL DRAWN OFF HERE

Hall-Heroult process The Hall-Heroult process is the final stage in a method of obtaining pure ALUMINUM. The large-scale production of aluminum today was made possible by the discovery of this process in 1886, by the American, Charles Martin Hall. In the same year a young French scientist, Paul Louis Toussaint Heroult, discovered the same process in France. Today it is usually called the Hall-Heroult process in honor of both men.

Alumina, or aluminum oxide (Al_2O_3), is dissolved in a solution of molten CRYOLITE at a temperature of approximately 1800° F. (982.2° C.). The solution is in a carbon-lined steel tank inside an electric furnace. Large rods or blocks of carbon are suspended into the solution and an electric current is sent through it. The electric current causes the oxygen to be drawn to the positive poles, or the carbon rods. Carbon monoxide (CO) and carbon dioxide (CO_2) are formed. The pure aluminum settles on the bottom of the tank, the negative pole or ELECTRODE. The aluminum, which is now about 99.8% pure, is siphoned off the bottom of the tank.　　　J.D.B.

Halogen (HAL-uh-juhn) A halogen is any element belonging to a certain chemical family. The members of this family lack just one electron of having a closed outer shell of electrons. The family includes FLUORINE, CHLORINE, BROMINE, IODINE, and ASTATINE. All halogens show a negative oxidation number of 1 in compounds. They react with metals to form SALTS and with hydrogen to form acids.

SEE ALSO: ACIDS AND BASES, ELEMENTS, METAL, VALENCE

Hamster The golden hamster is an animal about 5 inches (12.7 centimeters) long with light brown fur. It belongs to the MOUSE group. It has pouches inside its cheeks which it fills with grain, fruit, seeds, insects, worms, and birds' eggs. When it finds a safe hiding place it empties the pouches by pushing against its neck and cheeks with its paws. The hamster's name comes from this habit of hoarding its food. In German *hamstern* means "to hoard."

Hamsters live in underground tunnels 4 to 5 feet (1.22 to 1.52 meters) below the surface, with many side chambers to store food. They sleep there in the day and come above ground at night to search for food.

The males and females live separately except during the mating season. They will attack fiercely if irritated. They produce newborn more often than any other mammal. They mate when 45 to 90 days old, and a litter of 2 to 15 is born 16 days later. They weigh 4 to 5 ounces (113 to 141 grams) and usually live about three years.

Golden hamsters make interesting pets

Courtesy Society For Visual Education, Inc.

Hamsters are valuable for laboratory work, for they reproduce quickly and have practically no diseases of their own.

Hamsters make interesting pets. When tamed they are very gentle. Hamsters are not native to the Western Hemisphere.

The *golden* or *Syrian* hamster is new to America. A single litter was found in Aleppo, Syria, in 1930. It was raised at Hebrew University in Jerusalem. The next year it was brought to England and in 1938 was shipped to the United States for use as a laboratory animal.

There are many species of hamsters. The *common* or *black* hamster found in Europe and Asia is the largest, about 9 inches (22.86 centimeters). Small species found in Greece and Central Asia are gray. P.G.B.

SEE ALSO: RODENTIA

Hangar see Aviation

Hansen's disease see Leprosy

Hard water see Water

Hardening of the arteries see Arteriosclerosis

Hardness scale The Mohs Hardness Scale is a table of ten MINERALS used by scientists in measuring hardness of materials.

These ten minerals represent graduating degrees of hardness. The DIAMOND which can be scratched by no other mineral has hardness 10 and TALC which can be scratched by all represents hardness 1.

A mineral can scratch anything equal to or below itself in hardness. Therefore, if a material can scratch GYPSUM No. 2 and be scratched by CALCITE No. 3, it is said to be of hardness 3. It could also be hardness 2, but the highest number is used for its description. J. M. C.

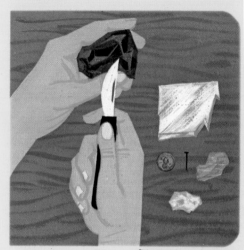

✳ **THINGS TO DO**

HOW HARD IS A MINERAL OR ROCK?

Materials: piece of glass, penny, pin, knife, quartz, topaz, and your own fingernail will be used.

1 Any rock which can be scratched with your nail has a hardness of one or two on the scale.

2 Minerals that can be scratched with a penny or pin are number three on the scale.

3 A knife scratches those with a hardness of four or five.

4 Minerals on the scale at six and seven will scratch glass.

5 Number eight on the scale will scratch quartz and nine will scratch topaz.

6 The diamond, number 10, will scratch all other rocks plus itself.

7 Using the hardness scale enables the rock hound to determine which minerals he has found on the trail.

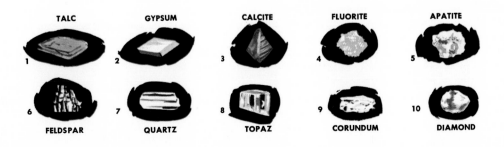

TALC 1   GYPSUM 2   CALCITE 3   FLUORITE 4   APATITE 5

6 FELDSPAR   7 QUARTZ   8 TOPAZ   9 CORUNDUM   10 DIAMOND

All pictures American Forest Products Industries, Inc.

White oak, a hardwood that takes a high polish

Black walnut, a hardwood that produces an edible nut

European ash, which has a tough, straight-grained wood

Hardwood Trees are divided into two groups: hardwood and SOFTWOOD. All coniferous (cone-bearing) trees are considered softwood, and all deciduous trees (that shed leaves) are hardwood. This standard has been applied to all the forests of the world by a committee of the United Nations.

Deciduous trees drop their leaves in fall; conifers are evergreen throughout the year. Forests of hardwood trees such as the birch and poplar may be found in the south of Siberia and Canada. In the United States and Central Europe are the hardwood forests of the temperate zone, such as the oaks, beeches, and maples. TEAK, MAHOGANY and EBONY trees, are the most abundant of all vegetation in the hardwood forests of the tropics. These great trees are often called the *rare woods,* but only because of the difficulty of transporting them out of the areas in which they grow.

All of the great forests have had a great influence upon the progress of mankind. Much of man's future well-being and prosperity lie in the development and proper use of the great forests.

Many hardwood trees are used for shade and beauty. They help prevent soil EROSION and floods. Medicines are obtained from the roots, bark, leaves, or fruit of hardwood trees. FRUITS such as the apple, pear, plum, peach, apricot, and cherry, as well as beverages, maple syrup, maple sugar, and nuts, come from hardwood trees. They are important providers of shelter, fuel and paper products. Shipbuilding, cabinet-making, and many other professions depend upon wood furnished by the hardwood forests.

OAK is the most important of the temperate zone hardwoods. Oak wood is hard, tough, durable, resilient, and elastic. Its great strength and ability to resist heavy strain make it valuable for shipbuilding and all types of heavy construction. It takes a high polish for fine cabinetwork.

The MAPLE is one of the more important hardwoods. It is heavy, tough, compact, strong, and very hard, and it takes a fine polish. Maple is light brown with a dense, even grain and fine texture. It is one of the best woods for furniture, veneers, flooring, bowling alleys, and violins.

The BEECH is moderately hard, strong, and heavy, with a fine-grained, pink-brown wood. It is used for boxes, flooring, interior finish, toolhandles, fuel, and charcoal.

Teak is one of the most durable woods of the important commercial timbers of the tropics. It is hard and does not warp, split, or crack; it makes a valuable timber for general construction. It is also very resistant to decay and termites. The wood is yellow-brown and greasy to the touch. It is used for ships and boats, furniture, and greenhouses.

Mahogany wood is red-brown with a crooked grain. It is very heavy and strong—hard enough to resist indentations, yet easy to work, and it polishes and glues well. It is used for furniture, musical instruments, caskets, airplanes, and plywood.

Ebony is a black wood with brown stripes. It is very hard and heavy and has a fine grain. It takes a high polish and is used for cabinet making, piano keys, sporting and athletic goods.　　　　M. R. L.

SEE ALSO: ECONOMIC BOTANY, FOREST PRODUCTS

Hare see Rabbit

Harelip Harelip is a deformity such as a fissure (break or crack) of the upper lip. Those who have this deformity are born with it. Harelip is not a good name because it is sometimes miscalled hairlip. Also, it is not exactly like the fissure or cleft in the upper lip of the hare.

The cleft in a rabbit's upper lip is Y-shaped. It is situated exactly in the middle line, with one branch extending into each nostril. In humans the fissure is toward one side or the other, or there may be two, one on each side of the mid-line. Sometimes it is not very deep. Other cases may involve the upper part of the mouth; when so extensive it is called a *cleft palate*. Sometimes this deformity seems to run in families. The condition can be corrected by SURGERY, and this should be done as soon as the baby's strength permits.   H. K. S.

Harvest The gathering in of crops, or the reaping season, is the harvest. Mankind has always celebrated after a good harvest. The end of the Pilgrims' first successful harvest was the reason for the first Thanksgiving.

The successful farmer plans to harvest his crops just as early as possible, but not before the crop is mature enough to give the greatest yields of superior quality.

Farm machines have made it possible for many more acres of grain crops to be harvested per man than ever before. Farmers are able to maintain a high level of production in spite of serious shortages of help.

Promptness is important in harvesting and handling perishable fruit and vegetable crops. A day's delay may result in heavy losses, especially in hot sultry weather, where there is danger of storms, or in seasons when frosts are likely to occur.

Crops such as beans, peas, and sweet corn should be harvested as soon as they reach maturity. Tomatoes and muskmelons grown for distant markets, are harvested long before they reach maturity. Lettuce often becomes almost worthless in a day after the heads have formed, especially if the weather is hot.   M. R. L.

SEE ALSO: AGRICULTURE

Harvestman see Daddy longlegs

William Harvey, discoverer of the circulation of the blood

Harvey, William (1578-1657) William Harvey was an important English physician who, without the aid of a microscope, discovered the circulation of blood in the human body. This discovery is the very foundation of modern MEDICINE. Harvey's book *On the Motion of the Heart and the Blood* is often called the most valuable book in the history of physiology.

William Harvey was born in Folkstone, Kent, on April 1, 1578. He studied at Caius College, Cambridge, and at the University of Padua, Italy. After he received his doctorate, he returned to Saint Bartholomew's Hospital in London where he became a physician. He then was invited to become a lecturer at the College of Physicians and soon his practice grew to include such distinguished men as the Lord Chancellor, Francis Bacon, and later kings James I and Charles I.

In 1628 Harvey published his book in which he announced his great discovery of the CIRCULATORY SYSTEM after he had publically declared his views in his lectures to the College of Physicians. Needless to say, there was tremendous opposition to an idea so startling. As time passed, however, opposition died and glory was heaped upon Harvey. All Europe honored him.

Describing this distinguished physician, John Aubrey has written, "In person he was not tall, but of the lowest stature; round faced, olivaster complexion, little eyes, round, very black, full of spirits; his hair black as a raven, but quite white twenty years before he died."   D. H. J.

Hatchery A hatchery is a place for hatching EGGS, especially those of poultry or fish. The young animals are made to develop in and come out of the egg by natural or by artificial means such as incubation.

SEE: FOWL, INCUBATOR

Hawk Hawks are found all over the world. Not all hawks belong to the same family, but all are alike in structure and habit. All are BIRDS OF PREY, which means they are flesh eaters. They catch and hold their kill with their sharp talons or claws and tear it apart with their hooked beaks. They are skillful flyers, swooping to seize prey in mid-air or on the ground. Hawks see well both close and far away. They are usually barred or striped, with brownish or grayish backs and lighter undersides. Many have yellow legs. The male is smaller than the female. Nests are usually stick platforms built high in trees.

The *red-tailed hawk* belongs to a subgroup of the *Accipitridae* family. The members of this group are large, soaring hawks that feed on rodents. In the same family are the *bird hawks*. Their rounded wings and tails enable them to dodge through woodlands after small birds. The *marsh hawks* have long slender legs and light bodies. They nest and hunt in swamps. The *sparrow hawk* and *pigeon hawk* are small members of the FALCON family.   E. R. B.

Cooper's hawk (left) is a bird hawk and the red-tailed hawk is a buzzard hawk

Courtesy Society For Visual Education, Inc.

Hawthorne, or thorn apple, tree

Haworth, Sir Walter (1883-1950) The 1937 NOBEL PRIZE in chemistry was won by Walter Haworth and Paul Karrer. Haworth, an organic chemist, studied carbohydrates and Vitamin C.

Before Haworth began his research, organic chemists could determine the numbers of carbon, oxygen, and hydrogen atoms in carbohydrate molecules. In some cases these numbers were the same, although the sugars were different. Haworth demonstrated the structure of carbohydrate molecules. He showed that some sugars had a ring-like arrangement of carbon and oxygen atoms. Others had a chain-like arrangement. He developed a way to determine the chain lengths of certain sugars. His work with carbohydrates led to his research with Vitamin C (ascorbic acid). He synthesized it in the laboratory.   A.J.H.

Hawthorne The hawthorne tree has tiny, reddish fruits or apples called *haws.* It also has long spikes or thorns. Some people call it the *thorn apple* tree. There are several kinds of hawthornes. Most grow about 20 feet (6.1 meters) high. In late spring, hawthornes are covered with white or reddish flowers. The English call it the *Maytree.* The pilgrim ship, *Mayflower,* was named after it.

The hawthorne has very dense branches. It often grows wider than it is tall. It grows wild in woodland and meadow areas, and because of its ornamental shape, is in popular demand for landscape gardening. Glossy green leaves turn orange-red in autumn. The small fruit of many hawthornes remain on the tree most of the winter, providing food for birds and small animals. The fruit can also be made into jelly.

J. A. D.

Hay see Grasses

Hay fever The POLLEN or yellow dust from a weed called *ragweed* is blown through the air in late summer. The pollen makes some people sneeze and makes their eyes itch and water. This is called hay fever. Sometimes they sneeze from being near hay, flowers (such as goldenrod), or certain trees. There is actually no fever, or rise in body temperature, in hay fever; it is an ALLERGY rather than an infectious disease.

Traveling to a place where there is no ragweed helps a victim. Air conditioners with filters remove some particles from the air, and antihistamines can be taken to relieve some symptoms. If sufferers also have ASTHMA, they will need special medications and/or inhalants. P.G.B./E.S.S.

Haze Haze is caused by bits of dust and other impurities in the atmosphere. It can greatly reduce visibility.

Haze occurs when the lower layers of the atmosphere are stable and the small particles of dust and other impurities, except smoke, are suspended in the air. Much of the reduction in visibility near large cities is due to smoke from manufacturing plants or other industrial activities. When haze and smoke occur together with fog or low *stratus* clouds, the combination is called "smog." This occurs most often during a weather condition called "temperature inversion."

Haze is more noticeable when flying in aircraft. This is particularly true when it is combined with smoke over cities. H. S. G.

Hazelnut see Nuts

Headache A headache is a pain in the head. It is only a symptom of disease. It can be caused by a nerve inflammation, scalp muscle tension, pressure in the skull due to dilated blood vessels, or even a brain tumor.

SEE ALSO: BLOOD PRESSURE, MIGRAINE

Health see Malnutrition, Nutrition, Purification, Sanitation, Sewage disposal, Vitamin, Vitamin deficiency

✳ **THINGS TO DO**

CAN YOU MAKE YOUR HEART BEAT FASTER?

1 foot = .3 meter

1 First, you will need an instrument to hear your heart beating.
2 Join the ends of three two-foot pieces of rubber tubing to the three arms of a glass Y tube.
3 Put small metal funnels on the free ends of the tubing. This will serve as a stethoscope.
4 Have your partner hold two funnels tightly to his ears while you place the third funnel over your heart. Count the heart beats per minute by the clock.
5 Now run around the room for several laps.
6 Count your heartbeat again. What happens when you exercise strenuously?

Heart The heart is a pump-like organ which keeps the blood circulating in the body by contracting and then relaxing. The heart first develops as a thick muscular tube which becomes divided into rooms or chambers. The chambers are separated by valves that allow the blood to flow only in one direction. The vertebrates (animals with backbones) have two, three, or four chambers to their hearts.

The fish heart has two chambers, one thin-walled, the *auricle* or *atrium,* and the other thick-walled, the *ventricle.* Blood which has had food and oxygen taken out of it by the cells of the body, and has had waste products put into it also by the cells

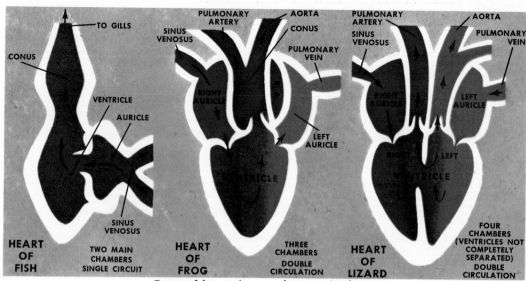

Types of hearts in some lower animals

is called *impure blood*. The impure blood is carried by the VEINS to the auricle of the heart. The auricle then contracts and sends the blood into the ventricle. When the ventricle contracts the blood is sent to the gills. In the gills the waste carbon dioxide is replaced by oxygen and the blood is now called pure or *purified blood*. The pure blood enters a large blood vessel (*dorsal aorta*) which branches and rebranches, carrying the blood to all parts of the body.

In the frog, a lung breather, the heart is three chambered because the auricle has become divided into two chambers. Impure blood from the body enters a receiving chamber for the heart (*sinus venosus*) which opens into the right auricle. Purified blood returns from the lungs to the left auricle through a vein (*pulmonary*). The auricles contract and the blood enters the ventricle. Impure blood coming in the right side of the ventricle, and pure blood coming in on the left, mix. Contraction of the ventricle sends the mixture into an artery (pulmocutaneous to both the LUNGS and skin) and into two arteries which join to become the dorsal aorta. Through this vessel and its many branches in the semi-purified arterial, blood is circulated through the body. The lung branch is smaller than the branch to the skin. More respiration occurs in the skin.

In some reptiles (snakes, lizards, turtles), the ventricle of the heart is beginning to be divided into two parts. Because of this there is less mixing of the two kinds of blood.

Among the birds and mammals, includ-ing humans, the heart is four chambered because the ventricle has become com-pletely divided into two separate chambers. There is no longer any mixing of pure and impure blood.

The human heart is one of the toughest organs in the body and is about the size of a clenched fist. It is covered by a thin membrane, the *pericardium*. Weighing a lit-tle less than ¾ of a pound (34 grams), the heart beats an average of 72 times a minute, with only a short rest between beats. In one hour the heart pumps the equivalent of about 520 quarts (492 liters) of blood, cir-culating all the blood through the body about 37 to 43 times.

When impure blood enters the human heart it enters the cavity of the right au-ricle, through two veins, one coming from the head region and one from the lower or posterior region of the body, (*superior and inferior vena cava*). At the same time puri-fied blood from the lungs enters the left auricle through the pulmonary vein. When the auricles contract, the *tricuspid* valve on the right and the *mitral* or *bicuspid* valve on the left open. Blood enters the ventricles through these open valves. When the ven-tricles contract, the tricuspid and mitral valves close. Strands of connective tissue from the inner layer of the heart (ENDO-CARDIUM) anchor the valves so that they do not open toward the auricles and let blood flow backwards. During the ventri-cular contraction the *semilunar* valves in

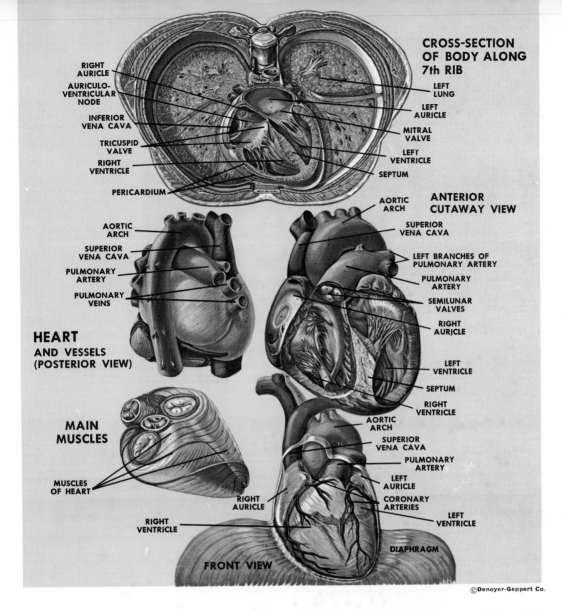

CROSS-SECTION OF BODY ALONG 7th RIB

RIGHT AURICLE
AURICULO-VENTRICULAR NODE
INFERIOR VENA CAVA
TRICUSPID VALVE
RIGHT VENTRICLE
PERICARDIUM
LEFT LUNG
LEFT AURICLE
MITRAL VALVE
LEFT VENTRICLE
SEPTUM

ANTERIOR CUTAWAY VIEW

AORTIC ARCH
SUPERIOR VENA CAVA
LEFT BRANCHES OF PULMONARY ARTERY
PULMONARY ARTERY
SEMILUNAR VALVES
RIGHT AURICLE
LEFT VENTRICLE
SEPTUM
RIGHT VENTRICLE
AORTIC ARCH
SUPERIOR VENA CAVA
PULMONARY ARTERY
LEFT AURICLE
CORONARY ARTERIES
LEFT VENTRICLE
DIAPHRAGM

HEART AND VESSELS (POSTERIOR VIEW)

AORTIC ARCH
SUPERIOR VENA CAVA
PULMONARY ARTERY
PULMONARY VEINS

MAIN MUSCLES

MUSCLES OF HEART

RIGHT AURICLE
RIGHT VENTRICLE

FRONT VIEW

©Denoyer-Geppert Co.

the pulmonary ARTERY and aorta open. Purified blood from the left ventricle passes into the aorta and is eventually distributed throughout the body. Impure blood in the right ventricle enters the pulmonary artery and goes to the lungs to exchange carbon dioxide for oxygen. The heart itself is supplied by coronary arteries branching off the aorta just as it leaves the ventricle.

In the human heart and in the hearts of a few other mammals, there is a special kind of excitable tissue called *nodal tissue*. It starts and regulates or controls the speed of the heartbeat. The most important node of muscular nervous tissue is located in the right auricle (*sino-auricular* node) and is known as the *pacemaker* of the heart. It continues as a band of muscular nervous tissue (*auriculo-ventricular* node or *Bundle of His*) down through the walls separating the auricles and the right and left ventricles. When the heart contracts, the wave of contraction starts in the pacemaker, goes through the walls in the auricles, and continues in the walls of the ventricles. The pacemaker is regulated neurally by the brain and autonomic nervous system. It is regulated chemically by salts dissolved in the liquid portion of the blood plasma and temperature changes. The amount of carbon dioxide in the blood also has an influence in regulating the pacemaker. The contraction and relaxation of the heart muscle creates a rhythmic cycle. The contracting portion of this cycle of the heart, the SYSTOLE, and the relaxation portion, the DIASTOLE, are followed by a short period of rest.   J. C. K.

SEE ALSO: BLOOD, BLOOD PRESSURE, CIRCULATORY SYSTEM, HEART MURMUR, TRANSPLANTS

Heart murmur Heart murmurs are unusual rushing sounds that the doctor hears when he or she listens to heartbeats through a stethoscope. Normally, two main sounds ("lubb-DUPP") are heard. There are no extra sounds or "murmurs" in between.

As blood is pumped through the heart, it must pass through four valves and chambers. If heart disease, blood disease, abnormal heart development, or a hole in the heart wall are present, they prevent the valves from opening or closing fully. The normal "lubb-DUPP" sound of the two major heart beats can change, or extra sounds or rushes of blood through damaged valves can be heard. These are *pathological* (abnormal) murmurs. They are usually quite loud, and they do not change much with the patient's position. Doctors use tests, such as X rays, EKGs, angiograms, phonocardiograms, and other laboratory tests (for anemia, for example) to pinpoint the location and extent of heart damage and to determine the cause of the murmur.

Thin people and children can have *functional* (normal) heart murmurs. Rushing sounds are heard in between the two main heart sounds. This comes from blood hitting normal heart chambers. These sounds are usually soft, and change when the patient's position or heart rate changes. A functional murmur is no cause for alarm.

A complete examination tells the doctor about the health of the heart, its nerves, valves, and muscles. The existence of a heart murmur is not a disease in itself. It merely indicates a change or changes that have occured in the heart and may not be normal. H.K.S./E.S.S.

SEE ALSO: CIRCULATORY SYSTEM, HEART

Heartbeat Heartbeat is the pulsation, or "beating," of the HEART. One heartbeat includes one full drawing-together and expansion of the heart muscles. This is one complete SYSTOLE and DIASTOLE.

SEE: CIRCULATORY SYSTEM

Heartwood Heartwood is the hard central part of trees. Botanists call heartwood "duramen."

Cross-section of a tree shows the heartwood

In a cross-section of a tree trunk, the center, or core, is darker in color than any of the outer part. This is the heartwood, or oldest XYLEM cells in the tree. The cells in the center are the farthest from the food conducting tubes, the PHLOEM. They become clogged with resin and other insoluble materials. This causes the cells to die, terminating their usefulness in conduction. However, heartwood provides support. The cells to the outside of heartwood (the outermost sapwood) are still alive. M. R. L.

SEE ALSO: PLANT TISSUES

Heat Heat is a form of energy essential to life. Without the heat energy from the sun, life could not exist on Earth. The sun warms the earth and makes things grow. When man eats food, some of it is turned into heat ENERGY to keep the body warm.

A hot stove or a bonfire has so much heat energy that one can feel it when he is close to the stove or fire. Many things seem cold because they have less heat energy than something hot. Even an ice cube has some heat energy. By taking more heat from it in a freezer, the ice becomes colder.

Temperature indicates how intense the heat energy is. It does not tell you how much heat the material has. For example, a school gym requires more heat to raise its temperature to 70° F. (21.1° C.) than a small room at home requires to reach the same temperature. Heat energy is measured in CALORIES in the Metric System or in B.T.U.'s (British thermal units).

In 1798, Count Rumford performed experiments proving heat is produced from mechanical energy. He observed that FRICTION from the drills used in boring cannon created tremendous quantities of heat. Because of Rumford's experiments, now we know that all other forms of energy,

✳ THINGS TO DO

WHAT MATERIALS WILL CARRY HEAT?

1 Hold one end of a metal rod. Place the other end in the flame of a candle. Will a solid, such as metal, carry heat?
2 Fill a pyrex bottle with cold water. Place it over a bunsen burner or on an electric plate. After five minutes feel the top part of the bottle. Will liquids, such as the water in the bottle, carry heat?
3 In the winter hold your hand above a radiator. What do you feel? Does air, a gas, carry heat?

Courtesy Society For Visual Education, Inc.

A calorie is the amount of heat needed to raise the temperature of one gram of water one degree Centigrade

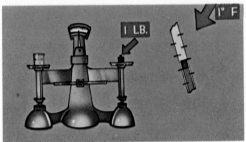

Courtesy Society For Visual Education, Inc.

A B.T.U. is the amount of heat needed to raise the temperature of one pound of water one degree Fahrenheit

such as mechanical or electrical energy, may be transformed into heat.

Heat energy is the total kinetic (moving) energy of the molecules of a substance. The KINETIC THEORY of matter states that all molecules possess this energy except at ABSOLUTE ZERO, which is −273.16° C. or −459.69° F. At that point molecular motion ceases, and molecules have no kinetic energy and therefore no heat energy. In solids and liquids, the kinetic energy of the molecules is reduced by the forces binding each molecule to its neighbor. To overcome these forces, heat energy must be added. For example, heat must be added to ice to convert it to water. In a similar fashion, large quantities of heat must be added to water to produce steam. If heat is added to the steam, the kinetic energy of each molecule is increased and the molecules move faster and farther away from each other.

The temperature of a substance is explained by the kinetic theory, too. Tempera-ture is proportional to the *average* kinetic energy of all the molecules of any body. A large stone and a small stone may have equal temperatures, but the large stone would have greater heat energy. The larger stone has more molecules, and the *total* kinetic energy of these molecules is greater than the total for the small stone, but the *average* kinetic energy in each is the same.

One is made aware of heat by its behavior. Any body at a higher temperature than its surroundings radiates heat to those cooler surroundings. Metals are good conductors of heat. The inside of a frying pan becomes hot because heat is conducted through the pan from the bottom. Heat may move from place to place by convection in liquids and gases. In a hot water tank, heat expands the water, which becomes less dense, and the cold water, of greater density, pushes the hot water to the top. Heat causes the EXPANSION of most solid substances as well as all gases.   A. E. L.

SEE ALSO: BRITISH THERMAL UNIT, HEAT BARRIER, HEAT OF FUSION, HEAT OF REACTION, HEAT OF VAPORIZATION, TEMPERATURE SCALES, THERMOCHEMISTRY, THERMOELECTRICITY

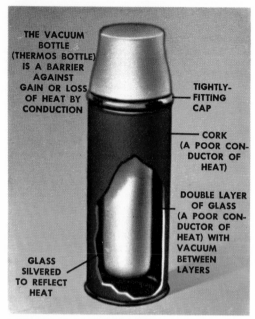

THE VACUUM BOTTLE (THERMOS BOTTLE) IS A BARRIER AGAINST GAIN OR LOSS OF HEAT BY CONDUCTION

TIGHTLY-FITTING CAP

CORK (A POOR CONDUCTOR OF HEAT)

DOUBLE LAYER OF GLASS (A POOR CONDUCTOR OF HEAT) WITH VACUUM BETWEEN LAYERS

GLASS SILVERED TO REFLECT HEAT

A heat barrier, such as in a thermos bottle, stops the transfer of heat

Heat barrier

A heat barrier is a material, often called an *insulator,* which surrounds a body or substance and enables it to retain heat. The retention of heat is often very desirable, especially in heating homes, in keeping food hot, and in keeping the body warm.

There are three ways in which heat is transferred from one place to another. They are: CONVECTION, which means literally "to carry with" and involves bodily transfer of the heated material; CONDUCTION, which means "leading with or along," in which heat is carried by a molecular transfer process; and RADIATION, which is somewhat similar to the propagation of light waves and also occurs with the same velocity

To stop the transfer of heat by any one of the above methods requires a different technique in each case. Since convection is the actual transfer of the heated material, the barrier must insure the retention of the heated body itself. In winter clothing, a woolen sweater or shirt usually creates a layer of motionless air which is heated by the body. This is then covered with a tight material, such as canvas or leather, to prevent any outside air from displacing the already heated air.

In the case where heat is lost through conduction, as in the walls of a home, the barrier is provided by actually constructing the walls from some material which is not a good conductor. Most metals are good conductors of heat. Cork, wood, glass, wool, or cloth are poor conductors. In general, a poor conductor is a good heat barrier.

Heat loss by radiation is one of the most difficult to prevent. All materials are radiators of heat, some to a lesser degree than others. Generally speaking, however, bodies which are light in color are poor radiators, and those which are dark in color are good radiators. Hence, if one wishes to reduce radiation, a white body would be chosen.

A. E. L.

SEE ALSO: ELECTRICITY, HEAT, INSULATION

Heat of fusion

Normally, when heat is supplied to a substance, the temperature of the material is raised. If, however, a pan of water and ice is placed over a flame and the mixture is carefully stirred until all the ice melts, no increase in temperature will be observed. The HEAT supplied has done something other than raise the temperature of the mixture.

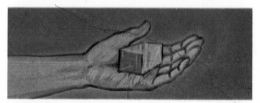

Melting ice feels cold because it absorbs heat

The temperature of melting ice is 32° F. (0° C.) and the temperature of water produced by melting ice is also 32° F.

All pictures courtesy Society For Visual Education, Inc.

It takes longer to boil water containing ice than it does to boil plain water

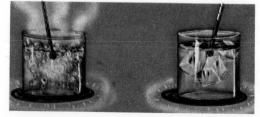

Slow, active and normal body states produce and give off heat due to chemical reactions

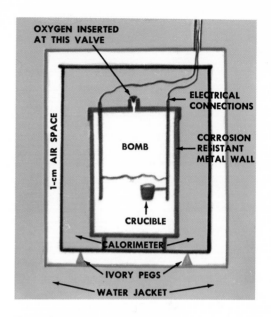

The calorimeter can be used to measure the heat of reaction produced by foods

The energy the heat supplied has actually been used to change the ice from water in the solid state to water in the LIQUID state. Each molecule has more ENERGY in the liquid form than in the solid form. The number of CALORIES necessary to change one gram of a substance from the solid state to the liquid state at a constant temperature is called the *heat of fusion.*

It requires 79.6 calories to convert one gram of ice at 0° C. (32° F.) to water without any increase in temperature. In the reverse process, 79.6 calories of heat must be removed from each gram of water before it becomes ice at the same temperature.

A.E.L.

SEE ALSO: PHYSICAL STATES AND CHANGES

Heat of reaction Heat of reaction is the quantity of HEAT which is given off or taken up when a chemical reaction takes place. The heat of reaction can be used to predict whether or not chemical reaction will take place.

When chemicals react and lose ENERGY to their surroundings, there are a number of ways in which the energy loss may occur. A mixture of hydrogen and oxygen will explode when ignited, some of the energy appearing as heat, some as light, and some as sound. In a few special cases a chemical reaction may proceed with the emission of light without the evolution of heat. A famil-

iar example is the reaction that occurs in the tail of the *firefly.* During most chemical reactions, however, energy is either lost or gained in the form of heat.

The experimental technique for measurement of the heat of reaction is based upon the concept that energy is conserved. This means that in a series of chemical reactions energy neither increases nor decreases in quantity but simply changes in form.

The device used for measuring heat of reaction is the CALORIMETER. The walls of a calorimeter are constructed so as to trap all the energy evolved by a chemical reaction carried out within the calorimeter. The heat of reaction is calculated from the temperature change. A temperature change is linked to a chemical change. The amount of energy required to change the temperature of the calorimeter reveals the total energy change of the reaction.

If, when the chemical reaction occurs, heat is given off, the reaction is *exothermic.* If heat is absorbed by the reacting system, the reaction is *endothermic.* If no heat energy is put into a system in which an endothermic reaction can occur, the reaction will *not* take place. For an exothermic reaction, however, no energy has to be added to the system from the outside for the reaction to occur. Therefore such a reaction can take place spontaneously.   J. R. S.

WATER AND GAS (STEAM) PRODUCED

Heat is used up when a liquid vaporizes to a gas

Heat of vaporization A liquid which is supplied with enough heat will increase in temperature until the BOILING POINT is reached. If further heat is supplied the liquid will convert to GAS, but no increase in temperature will be observed until all the liquid is in the gaseous state. The amount of heat which must be supplied to a unit mass of a material at its boiling point to convert it to gas at the same temperature is called the *heat of vaporization.*

Heat of vaporization and *heat of condensation* have the same value because the amount of heat is the same, but in the first case it is added, and in the second it is removed. The heat of vaporization for water is 970 B.T.U.'s per pound or 540 calories per gram.   A. E. L.

SEE ALSO: BRITISH THERMAL UNIT, CALORIE

Heather (HETH-er) Heather is a low-growing shrub that belongs to the genus *Calluna. Calluna* in Greek means "sweep." In ancient times the plant was used to make brooms. The common variety grows in masses, about 18 inches (45.72 centimeters) high. It has small evergreen leaves and small rosepink flowers. Heather is hardy and will grow on dry sunny slopes. It is raised for its foliage and flowers. It grows throughout Europe and Asia Minor.

Heather should be cut back in the spring to keep the plants compact and to keep them filled with flowering shoots. It blooms from July to October. It requires lime-free soils and plenty of leaf-mold or peat. New plants can be raised from cuttings of young shoots that are rooted under glass.   M.R.L.

Heavy hydrogen see Deuterium, Elements, Heavy water, Hydrogen

Heavy metals Heavy metals are metals five times as dense as water. These ELEMENTS are used in industry and are found in nature as *pollutants.*

The heavy metals are found on the periodic table between vanadium and germanium, zirconium and antimony, and lanthanum and, polonium. As a group these metals are considered poisonous.

Copper, mercury, and silver react readily with sulfur. They remove sulfur from protein in body cells, and the protein breaks down. The metals also attack sulfur-containing enzymes, thus blocking normal body processes.

Mercury is used in industry, in light switches and thermometers, and as a FUNGICIDE. This widespread usage has led to the release of much mercury into the environment. Many deaths have been attributed to mercury poisoning.

Once lead was used in paints. The paints were eaten by children and often caused deaths. Its use is now banned.   A.J.H.

Heavy water Heavy water is the common name given to the combination of an ISOTOPE of hydrogen and oxygen. This combination forms somewhat the same material as ordinary water. The scientific name for the isotope of hydrogen is DEUTERIUM, and the combination of deuterium and oxygen is called *deuterium oxide* (heavy water).

The heavy hydrogen isotope is given the symbol H^2 or D. The oxide then has the formula H^2_2O or D_2O, as opposed to H_2O for ordinary water.

Deuterium is used in many fields of scientific investigation, including physics, chemistry, biology, and mainly for the study of atomic nuclei.   A. E. L.

SEE ALSO: NUCLEAR SCIENCE

Hedgehog see Insectivore

Heidelberg man see Evolution of man

Heimlich's Choke Maneuver This is a method of saving someone who is choking on a piece of food lodged in the windpipe, which prevents normal breathing.

A person who is eating and suddenly starts to gag, cannot talk, turns blue, and loses consciousness may be suffering the so-called "cafe coronary." The rescuer first administers a few sharp blows to the victim's back, then puts his arms around the victim from behind, presses a fist into the victim's abdomen just below the center of the rib cage, and makes several sharp upward thrusts. This slides the food to where it can be pulled from the victim's mouth, allowing him to breathe again.   E.S.S.

SEE ALSO: ARTIFICIAL RESPIRATION, FIRST AID

Helicopter The helicopter is an aircraft that can rise straight up and hover in the air. It can also fly backwards or sideways. Instead of wings, helicopters use large, propeller-like *rotors* to lift them.

The helicopter was developed to do things no other aircraft can. A helicopter can move in any direction and can land or take off in small clear areas or on rooftops. For these reasons, helicopters are used for rescue, mail and passenger transportation, pipeline and electrical line inspection, and police work. Farmers use helicopters for spraying insecticides and fertilizer. They even use the downward draft from the rotor blades to circulate warm air through fruit orchards to prevent frost damage.

Helicopters are very useful for many jobs. These aircraft are flown for highway traffic control, to carry passengers, pipeline inspections, and many other interesting uses. *Heli-*

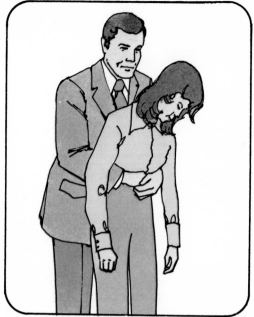

Heimlich's Choke Maneuver: After giving a few sharp blows between the shoulder blades, put arms around the victim, place fist just below the center of the rib cage, and press upward sharply a few times.

ports are often built on roofs of buildings.

The more powerful turbojet engines have made several advanced designs possible. Ten-ton (9-metric ton) loads can be picked up by the giant sky crane. The fixed rotor design has the rotor blades firmly attached to the hub for greatly increased stability.

Compound helicopters have a forward propulsion system, such as a pusher propeller or auxiliary jet engines, for speeds up to 300 miles (483 kilometers) per hour. Research is under way to develop a *composite aircraft*. Stub wings will provide basic lift in forward flight, while the rotor blades are stopped, folded, and stowed until needed.

HELICOPTER CONTROL

The flight control system of a helicopter is quite complex. The *cyclic pitch control* stick is located between the pilot's knees. It is used to direct the helicopter's hoizontal movements. This movement, in the same direction as that of the stick, is accomplished by varying the *pitch* or angle of the individual rotor blade so that the blade moving in the desired direction of flight takes a smaller "bite" of air, while the opposite blade takes a bigger "bite" and pushes the helicopter forward. As the blades rotate, their individual pitch is constantly changing.

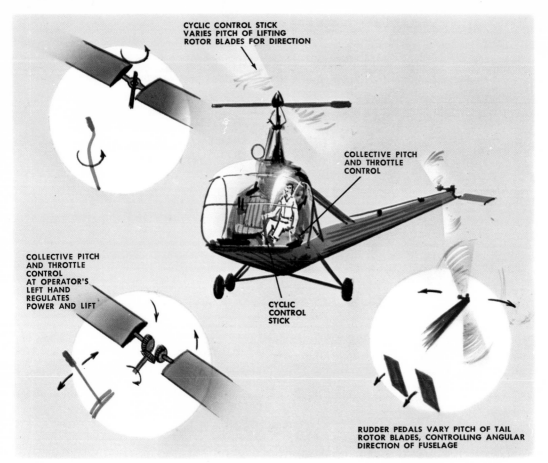

CYCLIC CONTROL STICK
VARIES PITCH OF LIFTING
ROTOR BLADES FOR DIRECTION

COLLECTIVE PITCH
AND THROTTLE
CONTROL

COLLECTIVE PITCH
AND THROTTLE
CONTROL
AT OPERATOR'S
LEFT HAND
REGULATES
POWER AND LIFT

CYCLIC
CONTROL
STICK

RUDDER PEDALS VARY PITCH OF TAIL
ROTOR BLADES, CONTROLLING ANGULAR
DIRECTION OF FUSELAGE

The *collective pitch control* is another "stick" at the pilot's left side. This controls the vertical direction of flight by varying the pitch of both rotor blades at the same time. The engine *throttle* is also located on this control stick. The raising of this stick giving increased pitch to the rotor blades is combined with speeding up the engine causing the helicopter to rise. To descend, the blade pitch is decreased by lowering the stick and at the same time reducing the engine power.

Two foot pedals are used to control the pitch of the small tail rotor blades. This pitch change has the same effect on the helicopter's flight as the rudder of a conventional aircraft in controlling right or left movement about the yaw axis.

If a helicopter's engine stops, the blades keep turning like a falling maple seed, and the aircraft settles to a safe landing. This is called *autorotation*.

Helicopters may have piston, turbojet, or ramjet ENGINES. Piston and turbojet engines turn the rotors through gears in much the same way as an airplane's propeller is turned. Ramjets may be mounted on the rotor tips, or the exhaust of a turbojet may be released from tubes in the tips.

The helicopter is not a new idea. Leonardo da Vinci made the first sketches, and Igor I. Sikorsky built the first practical helicopter in 1939. Powerful turbojet engines have made several advanced helicopter designs possible, including the high-speed *compound helicopter* and the giant *sky crane*.

Interesting research is under way to develop a composite aircraft which will use rotor blades to take off and land. In forward flight, this aircraft will use stub wings to provide basic lift. The rotor blades will be stopped, folded, and stowed until required for the landing operation.   R. J. J.

SEE ALSO: AIRCRAFT, AUTOGIRO

Heliograph Heliograph is a device with a moveable or shuttered mirror which can send messages over long distances by reflecting beams of sunlight in flashes.

Heliotrope

Heliotrope Heliotrope is one of the many plants of the *Borage* family. It produces clusters of small, fragrant, white to reddish-purple flowers, and is popular as a garden and pot plant. The name is often given to any plant which quickly turns toward the sun.

Heliotropism see Tropism

Helium Helium is a colorless, odorless gas. It is the second lightest of the elements, yet is twice as heavy as hydrogen, the lightest element. It has the simplest atomic structure of the elements. It is unusual since no one has yet succeeded in combining it with any other element, or even in grouping its atoms into molecules. It seems to be truly an *inert,* or unreactive, element.

Helium was discovered in the sun's spectrum in 1868 by Pierre Janssen during an eclipse. Its name comes from the Greek word *helios* meaning "the sun." Sir Joseph Lockyer identified it as an element, and in 1895 Sir William Ramsey first isolated it on earth. In 1907 Sir Ernest Rutherford first associated it with emanations of radioactive substances. Radium, uranium, and other naturally radioactive elements continuously give off *alpha particles,* which are the electrically charged nuclei of helium atoms.

Helium is scarce on Earth but the stars are composed chiefly of helium and hydrogen. Helium is derived from NATURAL GAS, but it can also be produced artificially. This helium nucleus consists of two protons and two neutrons, giving it a mass of four units and a charge of two units. The normal helium atom has its nucleus surrounded by a negative cloud containing two electrons.

Helium liquefies at $-268.9°$ C. ($-452.02°$ F.), and solidifies at lower temperatures under great pressure. These qualities make liquid helium useful in producing near absolute zero temperatures ($-273.16°$ C. and $-459.69°$ F.) for experimentation. The liquid helium readily passes through microscopic openings and seems to defy gravity as it creeps up the sides and over the edges of its container. Because its heat conductivity is almost a million times that of conventional liquids, it does not boil under intense heat. It evaporates.

Helium (symbol He) is element number 2. It has an atomic weight of 4.0026. It is an excellent heat conductor and so is used around high-voltage switches, to prevent metals from burning in heliarc welding, and to cool machinery.   D.C.H.

SEE ALSO: AIRSHIPS; ELEMENTS; RAY, ALPHA

Helldiver see Grebe

Hematite (HEMM-uh-tite) Hematite is the most important iron ore in the United States and one of the most common minerals. Its name means "bloodlike" because when scratched it shows a red streak.

Hematite (Fe_2O_3) appears in many varieties. Black CRYSTALS found in England are carved for use in rings. The shiny flakes of specular hematite grow together to form the famous "iron roses" found in the Alps. Soft, powdery hematite is called *red ochre* and is used as a paint pigment.

Almost all of the world's iron and steel comes from hematite. Tremendous commercial deposits in this country are located around Lake Superior and in Missouri and Alabama.   J. M. C.

SEE ALSO: IRON, ORE, STEEL

Hemisphere see Earth

Hematite is the most important ore of iron. When scratched it shows a red streak

Courtesy Society For Visual Education, Inc.

Small, round cones hold the seeds of hemlock

Hemlock Hemlock is an evergreen tree with cones. It grows mostly in forests, in ravines, and on rocky slopes. The leaves of a hemlock are short, flat NEEDLES. The needles are dark green on top and silvery colored underneath. The needles have a life span of about three years.

The reddish-brown cones are about ¾ of an inch (1.9 centimeters) long and hang on short stems. The cones open late in winter and release tiny seeds with wings about twice the length of the seed.

The eastern hemlock grows from Nova Scotia south to Alabama and west to the Great Lakes. The western hemlock, found from Alaska to California, is used for pulpwood and lumber. Hemlock bark is used in tanning leather. One species of hemlock which grows in southeastern states grows to be 100 feet (30.5 meters) tall. Hemlock wood is reddish brown.   P.G.B.

Hemoglobin see Blood

Hemophilia (hee-moh-FEEL-e-yuh) Hemophilia is an inherited disorder of the body. The blood of a person with this disorder takes longer to clot than it should. People who have hemophilia bleed freely after a slight injury, and sometimes they bleed without any apparent reason.

Bleeding into joints or from slight cuts may be serious and even result in death. The lack of blood clotting is due to the absence of the *antihemophilic globulin* factor (AHG) in the blood. Transfusion of AHG may stop the bleeding. True hemophilia is rare in females. However, it is a disorder carried by women and transmitted to sons. Such conditions of inheritance are *sex linked*.

This means they are defects carried in the X or female CHROMOSOME. In some cases, there appears to be no family history of the disease. It is likely that the trait has been passed from female to female for generations until eventually it develops in a male. Queen Victoria was a carrier and, through her children, passed the disease to the ruling families of Russia, Germany, and Spain.   B. M. H.
SEE ALSO: BLOOD, BLOOD TYPES, HEREDITY, MUTATION

Hemp Hemp is a plant. It is used to make rope, twine, yarn, and paper products. It has long stems, from 6 to 9 feet (1.8 to 2.7 meters) high. The stems are soaked in water and left outside to rot, then crushed and beaten to separate the fibers from the other plant cells.

Hemp is an annual plant, grown from seed. Some plants produce pollen, or *staminate,* flowers, and others produce ova and are the *ovulate* flowers. Pollen flowers are yellowish-green. Ovulate flowers bloom later and are not so colorful. When the flowers die the stalks are cut down. Hemp plants need a wet, mild climate.

Hemp seeds contain oil used in paints and varnishes and in making soap. MARIJUANA, a drug banned by law, also comes from the sap of the hemp plant. For this reason hemp growers in the United States must have a permit to cultivate the crop.

Manila hemp, or *abaca,* is not a true hemp. Manila rope has been made from abaca since the sailing ship days of the 1800s. Abaca fibers are tough and light and can be obtained in lengths from 6 to 12 feet (1.8 to 3.7 meters).   P.G.B.

Hen see Chicken, Fowl

Hench, Philip (1896-1965) The 1950 NOBEL PRIZE for physiology and medicine was shared by Philip Hench, Edward Kendall, and Tadeus Reichstein. They researched adrenal cortex hormones and discovered *cortisone.*

Philip Hench was an American physician. While on the staff of the Mayo Clinic in Rochester, Minnesota, he treated patients suffering from rheumatoid ARTHRITIS. In time he observed that rheumatoid arthritis patients had relief from their symptoms during pregnancy or jaundice. He theorized that this was due to the increase of female sex hormones during pregnancy and the increase in bile acids during jaundice. He worked with Kendall, a physiologist, in isolating these steroid hormones. In 1948 Hench began clinical experiments with cortisone. He proved that cortisone was an effective agent in relieving the joint inflammation due to rheumatoid arthritis.   A.J.H.

Henry, Joseph (1797-1878) Joseph Henry was one of the greatest physicists in the history of American science. He made important discoveries in the field of electromagnetism. His researches laid much of the groundwork for the development of the TELEGRAPH, TELEPHONE, RADIO, and DYNAMO. He was also the founder of the United States Weather Service.

Henry became interested in electromagnetism. His first important work was the development of the ELECTROMAGNET, which had been invented by William Sturgeon. Henry was the first to insulate wire for the magnetic coil, and he invented the "spool" or "bobbin" wire winding. Henry also found a way of producing an electric current by moving a MAGNET through a coil of wire. He did not publicize his discovery of induced current, however, until after MICHAEL FARADAY announced the same discovery in London. Faraday was given credit for the discovery, but in recognition of Henry's work the unit of electric inductance is now called by his name: a *henry*.

In 1832 Joseph Henry was appointed professor of natural philosophy at Princeton University where he continued his research in electromagnetism. In December of 1846, he was elected secretary of the Smithsonian Institution in Washington, D.C.

Henry had always been interested in meteorology. He realized the great need for more information, and one of the first things he did as secretary of the Smithsonian Institution was to organize a group of volunteer weather observers. The movement spread across the continent. He introduced standard instruments, and for

Joseph Henry

thirty years he laid the foundation for the science of meteorology.   D.H.J.

Hepatica see Wild flowers

Hepatitis (hepp-uh-TYE-tiss) Hepatitis is a disorder of the LIVER. In hepatitis, the liver becomes large, tender, and inflamed. An afflicted person loses his appetite or vomits, and his skin and eyeballs turn yellow (jaundice).

Toxic hepatitis is due to a poison, an inhaled gas, or a chemical. It is not contagious. Cleaning fluids and glue may cause it, particularly when used without adequate ventilation. *Infectious hepatitis* is caused by a virus that enters the body through the mouth. The virus exists in sewage-contaminated waters and can be transmitted by drinking contaminated water, eating shellfish that lived in such water, or by touching anything on which the virus lives. Treatment includes rest and a nourishing diet. People who have shared toilet facilities with a hepatitis patient are given gamma globulin to try to protect them from the contagious disease.

Serum hepatitis is caused by a similar virus, so-called because it was spread from the blood of one patient to another, either by transfusion or by a dirty hypodermic needle (as when passed among drug addicts). It has been found that the virus can also be passed on *venereally* (through sexual contact). A blood test has been developed that shows a particular antigen in the blood of donors who have had hepatitis, so that the contaminated blood will not be used for transfusions.   E.S.S.

SEE ALSO: JAUNDICE, LIVER

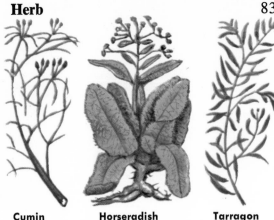

Cumin   Horseradish   Tarragon

Herb (HERB) A plant which does not grow a woody stem is an herb. Its stem is usually green, tender, and watery. That part of the plant above the ground dies down each year or growing season. Most monocotyledons and many dicotyledons are herbs. All other plants are shrubs or trees.

Herbs are composed of primary tissue. If vascular cambium is present, it lasts for only one year. Some plants have a perennial underground stem or rootstock, but the part above the soil line is herbaceous.

Many herbs are used in cooking, for they add flavor and aroma to foods. The seeds, dried leaves, or fresh leaves are the parts of herbs most often used as seasonings. Basil leaves add flavor and aroma to vegetables and salads. Thyme, sage, and chive add flavor to meat. True VANILLA flavoring is made from the fruit pods of the vanilla plant, an herb.

Herbage vegetables are plants whose parts aboveground are the storage areas. They have more minerals, proteins, and vitamins than carbohydrates. These are salad or pot herbs, such as asparagus and artichoke.

Herbalists, scientists during the fifteenth to seventeenth centuries, probably gave impetus to the modern study of plants. They located, described, and drew thousands of specimens.

Herbal is the general name for any book written by these early herbalists. They are about foods and medicine, and include such plants as cumin, horseradish, tarragon, and chive.

Herbicides are chemicals used to kill herbs. Those containing a high concentration of phenoxyl compounds destroy broad-leaved plants but not grasses.   H. J. C.

SEE ALSO: ECONOMIC BOTANY, PHARMACOL-
OGY, PLANTS, STEMS

Herbaceous (her-BAY-shuss) Herbaceous means "like an herb" or "having the appearance of a leaf." It refers especially to the presence of green coloring.

SEE: LEAVES

Herbarium (her-BARE-ee-um) A herbarium is a collection of dried plants. It is a record of the different kinds of plants from all parts of the world. Herbarium is also the name of the building in which these plants have been classified and displayed.

Herbicide (HERB-i-side) Chemicals that are used to kill plants are called herbicides. These poisons are often sprayed or dusted on unwanted plants to protect crops. However, if herbicides are not used wisely they can also kill animals and pollute air, water, and food.

There are close to 100 different chemicals commonly used today. Some are BIODEGRAD-ABLE, which means they will decompose in a few months. Others remain for years. Two common herbicides are 2,4-D and 2,4,5-T. They contain *auxin,* a hormone normally produced by plants. An excessive amount of auxin increases the respiratory activity faster than photosynthesis. A plant dies from growing so rapidly. This occurs in broadleaf plants such as weeds in a lawn. However, there is evidence that these herbicides are causing birth defects in humans.

During wars, whole ECOSYSTEMS are *defoliated* (the killing of leaves) with herbicides. The countryside is stripped of vegetation and ruined.   H.J.C.

Herbivore (HERB-ih-vor) Herbivores are *plant-eating* animals. Although most animals eat some plants, herbivores eat nothing but plants.

Since plants do not fight back when eaten, herbivores are usually gentle. However, all herbivores are food for flesh-eating animals. Since they are poorly equipped for fighting, many are swift runners. Others, like some insects, have protective coloring, which enables them to hide from their enemies.

Most hoofed animals eat plants. HORSES, COWS, ZEBRAS, and SHEEP graze on fresh or dried GRASSES. GIRAFFES and ELEPHANTS eat leaves. In fact, elephants can eat entire branches. The HIPPOPOTAMUS and MOOSE eat water plants like the water lily. In the TUNDRA regions, the CARIBOU paw the ground to find mosses and lichens.

Most gnawing animals or rodents eat smaller plants. While some, like the BEAVER and PORCUPINE, gnaw the bark of trees, the RABBIT nibbles at green clover and lettuce. SQUIRRELS search for mushrooms, seeds, nuts, and berries. Most insects are herbivores. They have mouth parts for tearing tissue or sucking juices. A few marine animals feed on plants. The CHITON has a mouth piece which shaves off plant tops.

Although plants are plentiful, they are not easy to digest. Herbivores must have special body parts for crushing tough, fibrous tissue and thick CELLULOSE walls. Many herbivores have broad, sharp-edged molars for grinding. Rodents have two pairs of incisor teeth which act like chisels for scraping plant tissue. Most herbivores have long intestines. These long intestines allow more time for digestion and more surface for absorption. Also, herbivores must eat more and eat more often than any other type of animal. E.P.L.

SEE ALSO: ARTIODACTYLA, BALANCE OF NATURE, CARNIVORE, DIGESTIVE SYSTEM, OMNIVORE, PROTECTIVE COLORATION, RODENT

Hercules

Hercules (HER-cue-leez) Hercules is a group of stars that resembles a man kneeling. The Greeks named it Hercules in memory of a very strong hero. In the summertime this CONSTELLATION can be seen nearly overhead. The main stars make a figure somewhat like a D in reverse or a crooked H, but some ancient peoples thought it looked like a butterfly.

Hercules, the ancient Greek hero, was supposed to be one of the strongest men who ever lived. He performed tremendous feats. Greek mythology tells many stories about the powers of Hercules. He was famous for twelve specific feats, which are called the "twelve labors of Hercules." One

Constellation Hercules

of these labors was killing the dragon that guarded the golden apples in the Garden of the Hesperides. The dragon is immortalized in the sky in the constellation DRACO, which is near Hercules. Ancient star maps picture Hercules with one foot on the head of Draco.

In the constellation Hercules there is a very famous cluster of stars. On a clear night it may look like a small fuzzy patch, but with a telescope it can be seen to consist of thousands and thousands of stars.

C. L. K.

Heredity

Heredity (huh-RED-uh-tee) The study of the ways in which physical traits are passed from one generation to another is heredity. A geneticist is a scientist who studies heredity. He is interested in the ways young plants or animals resemble (look like) their parents and in the ways they do not resemble them. A boy may have brown hair like his father's, but he may have blue eyes instead of brown eyes like his father's.

Eye and hair color are examples of what a geneticist calls *physical* characteristics or traits. A geneticist is also interested in *how* the boy got the brown hair like his father's and why his eyes are of a different color.

The passing or transmitting of traits from one generation to another (parents to children or to grandchildren) is called *inheritance*. The uniting of an EGG cell from a female (mother) with a SPERM cell from a male (father) produces a new individual—a young child, animal, or plant. Egg cells and sperm cells are called *germ cells*. The only real connection between two generations is through the germ cells. Therefore, inheritance of a characteristic such as hair color must be transmitted by these cells.

MENDEL'S EXPERIMENTS

In 1865 GREGOR MENDEL, an Austrian monk, published the results of his study of inheritance in the common garden pea. He discovered, after mating hundreds of peas, that some traits are strong or *dominant* and other traits are weak or *recessive*. When tall peas were mated or crossed with short peas, the offspring—the peas of the first generation—were not of middle height but were all tall like the tall parent. Tallness in peas is stronger than, or dominant to, shortness. Shortness is called the *recessive* characteristic because it does not show or remains covered for one generation.

When the tall peas of this first generation were mated, their offspring, the second generation, were both tall like their parents and one grandparent, or short like the other grandparent. There were three times as many tall plants as short ones, a proportion or ratio of 3:1. All of the short plants when mated with other short plants had only short offspring. One third of the tall plants when mated with other tall plants had only tall offspring. In the words of a geneticist, these plants *bred true to type*. When the remaining two thirds of the tall plants were mated or crossed with one another, the offspring were again both tall and short in the same proportion as before, three talls to one short.

Flower color, seed color, and other characteristics were found by Mendel to be inherited in the same manner. Later, the Mendelian principles of inheritance were found to hold true for animals. Many human characteristics are now known to be dominant over others. For example, dark eyes are dominant over blue, and dark hair over blond.

RELATIONSHIPS BETWEEN CHROMOSOMES, GENES AND MENDELIAN INHERITANCE

For many years, scientists have been interested in finding out how the germ cells transmit characteristics and how the ratios described by Mendel are produced.

The nucleus of a cell contains pairs of CHROMOSOMES, their number being constant for any given species. The cells of man contain 23 pairs, the cells of the FRUIT FLY contain four. Germ cells contain one chromosome from each of the pairs because they undergo a special division (*meiosis*) in which the chromosomes of each pair separate, each entering one of the two egg or sperm cells resulting from the division. After fertilization, the cell formed is known as a ZYGOTE, and it again contains the total number of chromosomes constant for the species.

Chromosomes are made up of many small chemical units or areas called *genes*. These are believed to be responsible for transmitting hereditary characters. Any given GENE almost always occupies the same place on a chromosome. Both the genes on a pair of chromosomes may be alike and act to produce the same trait, as the tallness in peas. They may be unlike, one acting to produce tallness, the dominant trait, and the other capable of producing short peas

The banded chromosomes in a fruit fly may be seen with a microscope

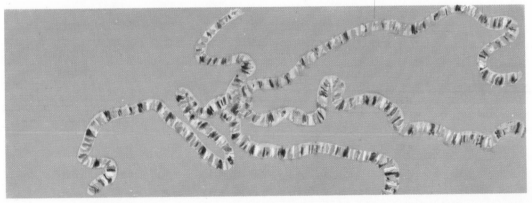

when its action is not suppressed or stopped by a dominant partner. A pair of genes such as these (one for tallness and one for shortness) are called *alleles* or *allelomorphs*. When a pair of genes are unlike, two kinds of germ cells are formed during meiosis. One type of germ cell will carry a chromosome containing the dominant gene for tallness, and another germ cell will carry the gene for shortness on the other chromosome of the pair.

SYMBOLS AND DIAGRAMS COMMONLY USED BY GENETICISTS

Geneticists have worked out a diagram to show the relationships between Mendel's inherited traits and the behavior of the chromosome pairs during the meiotic division of the germ cells. This diagram has become the standard way to represent mating between animals or plants without having to go into long wordy explanations.

The gene for tallness may be shown or represented by the capital letter "T". Shortness may be considered as the absence of tallness so its gene may be represented by a small letter "t". The symbol or sign used to show that two individuals have been crossed is an "X".

When short plants are crossed with tall plants, pollen from the short plant may be used to pollinate flowers of the tall. In this case *t-sperm X T-egg = (Tt)-zygote*. Pollen from tall plants may be used to pollinate flowers from short plants and may be diagrammed as T-sperm X t-egg = (tT)-zygote. In both of these cases the plants developing from the (tT)-zygotes will appear tall be-

cause of the dominant T-gene but will carry the t-gene on one of their chromosomes. Such (tT) individuals are known as *heterozygotes* because they carry genes for height which are not alike. If the genes for height are alike as in a (TT)-zygote, the individuals are known as *homozygotes*.

When the germ cells of a (tT) individual undergo meiosis, there will be produced two kinds of eggs and two kinds of sperm. These are t-sperms, T-sperms, t-eggs, and T-eggs. In genetics a checkerboard type of diagram is used to show the possible combinations of these genes in the zygotes formed through fertilization.

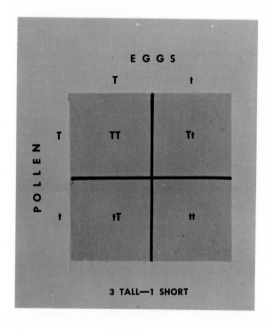

Mendelian inheritance of characteristics as shown in garden peas

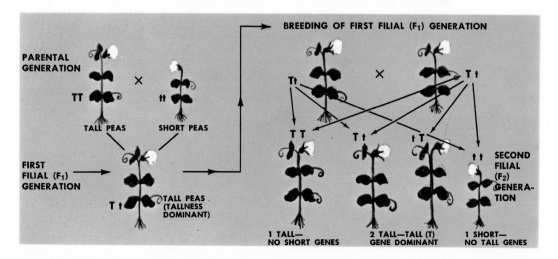

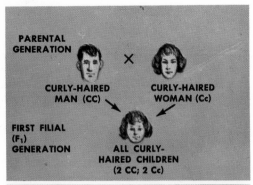

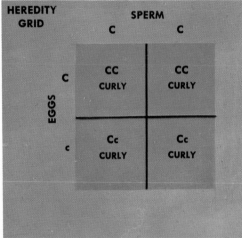

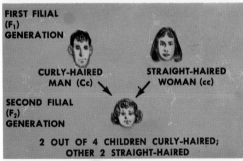

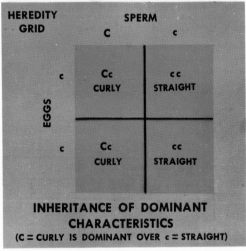

INHERITANCE OF DOMINANT CHARACTERISTICS
(C = CURLY IS DOMINANT OVER c = STRAIGHT)

The checkerboard shows there are two kinds of plants, tall and short. There are three times as many tall plants as short ones, the expected ratio of 3:1. All the tall plants look alike and have the same *phenotype*. However, they are not alike in genetic make-up since some of them are (TT) and others (tT). When the plants are classified on the basis of their genetic formulas, they have different *genotypes*. In the above cross, the tall plants are of two genotypes, (TT) and (tT).

INHERITANCE OF SEX

Most of the genes for determining sex may be located on one of a pair of chromosomes. The males of some species of bugs *(Hemiptera)* have an unpaired sex chromosome. During meiosis, two kinds of sperm are formed, one kind having an extra chromosome, called the X-chromosome. The females have an even number of chromosomes so that all the eggs produced have an X-chromosome. During fertilization, an X-egg and an X-sperm form an XX-zygote which becomes a female. When one of the X-eggs is fertilized by a sperm without an X-chromosome, the zygote develops into a male. This type of sex determination is known as XX-XO type, with "O" referring to the absence of one chromosome.

In man and in the FRUIT FLY, there are the same number of chromosomes in each sex but the sex chromosomes are alike in the female (XX) and unlike in the male (XY). Therefore, there are two kinds of sperm cells, an "X" or a "Y", and only one kind of egg cell.

A third type of sex determination was discovered among the birds and moths. Here, there are two types of eggs. A female is (XY) and a male (XX).

SEX LINKAGE

Sex-linked inheritance refers to the transmission of genes, by the sex chromosomes, which do not themselves determine the sex. In man, bleeder's disease (HEMOPHILIA), night blindness, and red-green color blindness are sex linked. The gene for color blindness is recessive. Therefore, both X-chromosomes in the female must bear the gene in order to produce a color blind female. If the one X-chromosome in the male carries the gene for color blindness, the male will be color blind.

GENES AND EVOLUTION

Currently EVOLUTION is defined as any change in allele frequency or the appearance of genes. If traits remain basically the same generation after generation, organisms do not evolve into something different. Several factors cause changes in genes which then causes evolution.

Mutations occur about one in every 10,000 offspring of a species. Evolution would be a slow process if this were the only factor, particularly in higher animals where the gestation period is long and single births are common.

Another factor is cross breeding. Organisms of the same species, but from different geographical populations, can cause a *gene flow*. This affects the frequencies of certain traits, and these appear more often. This definitely speeds up the evolutionary process.

A third factor is called *genetic drift*. Gene frequency depends on the size of any population. The smaller the group of living organisms breeding with each other, the greater the chance of certain genes appearing again and again. It's like flipping a coin. If one flipped it five times, tails may appear five times. However, if it were done 100 times, the ratio of heads to tails would be closer to 50:50. Thus, when a mutation occurs within a small population, the chance of the change remaining is greater than in a large population.

Finally, natural selection plays a significant role. The more successful organisms reproduce more offspring. Their gene patterns are passed along. Some conditions affect natural selection, such as number of predators, diseases, and physical change in the environment.

Humans have the knowledge to change the directions of the evolution of plants and other animals, but do not have the power to stop it. It is a never-ending process that will continue as long as living creatures inhabit the earth.   H.J.C./J.C.K.

SEE ALSO: BREEDING, CELL, EGGS, EVOLUTION, FERTILIZATION, HYBRIDIZATION, MITOSIS AND MEIOSIS, REPRODUCTIVE SYSTEMS

Hermaphrodite (her-MAFF-ruh-dyte) A hermaphrodite is an organism containing *both* male and female sex organs. Lower forms of animal life, such as the EARTHWORM, snails, clams and other bivalves, are hermaphrodites. Higher forms of life, including humans, are rarely hermaphrodites. However, hermaphrodism is the normal state in the first few weeks of human embryonic life.

Hernia (HERN-ee-uh) A hernia is the thrusting out of a piece of tissue or an organ through a weakness in the body wall. The weakness has either existed since birth or results from an injury, strain, or surgical incision.

Three common types of hernia are *umbilical, inguinal,* and *femoral*. A bulge is noted by the affected person, sometimes after a sudden physical strain. This bulge is the peritoneum (the lining membrane of the abdomen) pushing out of the weakened abdominal wall. If a portion of the intestine is forced into this sac-like protrusion, the hernia can strangulate from loss of blood supply, and emergency SURGERY is necessary. To prevent this and to repair the abdominal defect, elective surgery is often done.   E.R.B./E.S.S.

Heroin see Morphine

Heron (HAIR-uhn) Three types of birds are found in the heron family. These are the herons, the EGRETS, and the BITTERNS. Most herons are sociable birds. They nest and roost together in large groups or flocks. During the day, while feeding, they are solitary. They return to the flock at night.

Herons inhabit the shorelines of rivers, lakes, inlets, or saltwater ponds. They feed upon frogs, crayfish, fish, and smaller reptiles. Herons all catch prey by spearing with their long, pointed bills. Some stand perfectly still until their prey gets close enough to spear; others wade carefully up to within spearing distance; still others run through the water trusting on their speed to capture prey before it escapes. Their noisy cries sound like hoarse squawks.

Young are born covered with downy filaments, and are raised in a nest. When being

fed, babies grasp the base of the mother's bill with their own while their parent regurgitates food into their mouths or into the nest. The long-legged herons belong to the family Ardeidae.   J. C. K.

Herring Fish in the herring family are usually less than 18 inches (45.7 centimeters) long. SARDINES, ALEWIVES, and SHAD are all in this marine family. There are more food fish in this family than in any other. They are silver, with scales that drop off easily.

Herschel, William (1738-1822) Herschel was the German astronomer and philosopher who discovered the planet URANUS. His research methods are still used.

Born in Hanover, Germany, Herschel moved to England in 1757 and for twenty-six years supported himself by giving organ lessons. At night he studied Greek, Latin, literature, and science. But Herschel's greatest love was ASTRONOMY.

In 1781, using a homemade telescope, Herschel discovered the planet Uranus, which he named for Urania, the muse of astronomy. This was the greatest discovery of astronomy since GALILEO had invented the telescope. The following year King George III appointed Herschel Royal Astronomer.

Later, using a larger telescope he had built, Herschel discovered two satellites of Uranus and two of SATURN. He also discovered a large number of double stars, nebulae, and clusters of stars.   D.H.J.

Atlantic herring is an important food fish
Chicago Natural History Museum

Hertz (HURTS) Hertz is the unit of measure for events that repeat themselves. When a ball is dropped to the floor, it bounces. The number of times a ball bounces up and down in one second is called its *frequency*. This is measured in Hertz.

The unit for frequency was cycles per second. Hertz has replaced cycles per second in most areas. Hertz (Hz) is named for Heinrich Hertz, who was the first to demonstrate the production and reception of radio waves. Kilohertz, megahertz, and gigahertz are common frequency multiples.   A.J.H.

Herzberg, Gerhard (1904-) Gerhard Herzberg won the 1971 NOBEL PRIZE in chemistry. Herzberg was a pioneer in the study of atoms and molecules with a SPECTROSCOPE.

Herzberg's research dealt with the measurement and interpretation of spectral bands produced by emission or absorption of light by molecules. His techniques, important in ASTROPHYSICS, are applied to the study of cosmic radiation. His work is also important in molecular chemistry.

Born and educated in Germany, he migrated to Canada. Working with the National Research Council of Canada, he established one of the world's best laboratories for the study of spectroscopy.   A.J.H.

Hess, Victor (1863-1964) The 1936 NOBEL PRIZE for physics was awarded to Victor Hess and Carl Anderson for discovering cosmic radiation. Hess was an Austrian who later became a U.S. citizen.

Hess researched radioactivity and the electrical conductivity of air. In his early work he studied the constant heat produced by radium. He also studied the effects of high altitude on *ionization*. He used balloon ascents in his research. He discovered that radiation increased at a one-mile (1.6-kilometer) altitude. He theorized that there was radiation coming from space. This radiation, later named cosmic radiation, became an important factor in atomic research.   A.J.H.

✳ **THINGS TO DO**

CAN YOU MAKE A FROG HIBERNATE?

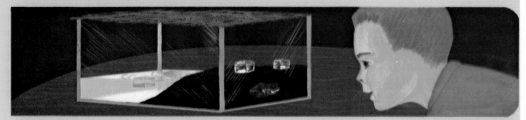

This experiment should be performed in the winter months or it can be done with ice cubes in the summer.

1 Assemble a semi-aquatic aquarium for an amphibian. One end should be a pool of water with a mud bank tapering up to land on the other end. Place a wire screen over the top of the container to prevent the frogs from jumping out.

2 Observe the activity of the frogs in a warm room, the pulsing of its throat as it breathes rapidly.

3 Transfer the aquarium to the cold outside for several hours. It may be placed in front of an open window in winter if the rest of the space around the aquarium can be blocked off.

4 Now observe the frog. Its breathing slows down, it becomes slow and sluggish, and starts to burrow into the mud bank. This is hibernation.

5 Adding ice cubes to the pool in the aquarium and scattering them over the aquarium will cause hibernation also.

Hibernation Many animals sleep or go into a "trance" during the long, cold winter months. This winter sleep is called *hibernation*. The bear is not classified as a true hibernator. Some animals that do hibernate include the badger, gopher, chipmunk, woodchuck, skunk, dormouse, prairie dog, squirrel, bat, toad, frog, and certain reptiles, insects and fishes.

Hibernators must get ready for the long period of inactivity. The animal needs to accumulate an excess of fatty tissue for use during the weeks or months that it is fasting. This stored fat will be converted into energy needed to keep the animal alive but not active. Hibernators will then select a protected spot away from enemies and the elements of the weather. During hibernation, all of the metabolic processes of the body are usually subnormal. The respiration rate is slow and irregular. The temperature of the body drops since the amount of heat produced is less. The heartbeat slows down. The woodchuck's heart, for example, beats only a few times per minute.

The hormones secreted by the endocrine glands are reduced. Almost every physiological process in some hibernators slows to a walk. Hibernation allows warm-blooded animals to live farther north than they would otherwise be able to.

The hibernation habits of animals seem to be passed on from their ancestors. There are some kinds of BEARS where the female hibernates and the male does not. Some caterpillars hibernate under moss or tree bark. They actually freeze and then thaw gradually in the spring. If the temperature gets warm suddenly, they usually die, as other animals may die if roughly wakened.

Some snails and other insects go into similar deep sleeps during a hot, dry summer. This sleep is called *estivation*.   H. J. C.

Hibiscus (hy-BISS-cuss) Hibiscus is the name of a group of shrubs and trees of the *mallow* family. Most of these plants grow in warm climates throughout the world. Types of hibiscus differ greatly in size, but all are known for their large, colorful flower.

The state flower of Hawaii is the flower of the Chinese hibiscus, a tree or tall shrub that grows to 30 feet (9.1 meters). This plant is frequently grown in greenhouses. The smaller swamp hibiscus, or swamp rose MALLOW, produces a pink flower 8 inches (20.3 centimeters) in diameter.

The tropical, yellow-flowered musk mallow is grown for seeds used in perfume and for flavoring drinks. South Sea islanders make wreaths of flowering hibiscus. OKRA, cultivated as a garden shrub, is more often grown for its long seed pods, which are eaten as a vegetable. J.A.D.

Hiccough (HICK-up) A hiccough is a periodic, sudden movement or contraction of the DIAPHRAGM. It is caused by an irritation of the nerve centers or pathways associated with the muscular diaphragm. Hiccoughs often accompany stomach disorders, illness or bad eating habits.

SEE: NERVOUS SYSTEM, RESPIRATORY SYSTEM

Hickory Hickory trees are large trees known for their nuts. Some have very rough, shaggy bark. They are slow-growing but tall trees found chiefly in central and eastern United States, One of the most popular of the trees is the *pecan*. The green wood creates a hot, slow-burning fuel used in giving meat a smoky flavor.

These hardy trees can reach heights of 120 feet (36.6 meters). They are slow to leaf in spring and show a dull, gold leaf in autumn when they shed their leaves. The wood is tough and elastic but decays if over-exposed. Wagon parts, skis, golf clubs, and tool handles are made of hickory. J.A.D.

SEE ALSO: NUTS

Hide see Leather

The hickory tree with full foliage

Courtesy Society For Visual Education, Inc.

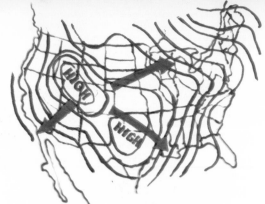

This weather map shows two high pressure centers, or areas of clear, dry weather

High-pressure center A high-pressure center is the center of a large air mass in which air pressure and temperature is about the same throughout the air mass. The name of this kind of air mass is *anticyclone,* or high. The word "cyclone" means "to whirl," and the winds of an anticyclone whirl in a counterclockwise direction. High-pressure air masses usually bring cooler temperatures and clearing skies. They move from west to east across the United States. H. S. G.

SEE ALSO: AIR MASS, CYCLONE, WEATHER FORECASTING

High fidelity One meaning of fidelity is exactness or accuracy.

In electronics, the exactness with which a piece of information is reproduced is a measure of fidelity. High fidelity, or "hi-fi," sound has been reproduced as faithfully as possible from the original. Some major parts or components of a hi-fi system are records, microphones, and speakers.

SEE ALSO: ELECTRONICS, SOUND RECORDING

Hill, Archibald Vivian (1886-   ) Hill is a British physiologist who shared the 1922 NOBEL PRIZE for physiology and medicine with Otto Meyerhoff. He researched heat production and the release of energy by muscles.

Hill's principal research investigated the production of *lactic acid* by muscle exercise and the resulting amount of energy produced. Dr. Hill has written extensively on the subject. P.P.S.

Himalaya Mountains see Asia

Hinge joint see Joints, skeletal

Hinshelwood, Sir Cyril (1897-)
The 1956 NOBEL PRIZE in chemistry was
won by Sir Cyril Hinshelwood and
N.N. Semenov. They studied chemical
kinetics. They studied rates and
mechanisms of chemical reactions.

Hinshelwood's early research dealt with
molecular kinetics. He investigated reaction
mechanisms, free radicals, chain reactions,
and energy requirements for chemical reactions. Later he worked with molecular
kinetics in living organisms, BACTERIA.
Hinshelwood's study of bacteria led to his
theory of resistance: bacteria can become
resistant to certain drugs after long
exposure to them.   A.J.H.

Hippocrates (hip-POCK-ruh-teez)
(460?-377? B.C.) Hippocrates was
the Greek physician whose oath is
still taken by medical students when
they graduate. The oath reads, in part,
"I swear . . . so far as power and dis-
cernment shall be mine, I will carry
out regimen for the benefit of the sick
and will keep them from harm and
wrong. To none will I give a deadly
drug even if solicited . . . Into what-
soever house I shall enter I will go for
the benefit of the sick."

Before Hippocrates, medicine was practiced according to superstition and myth.
Hippocrates did not believe that sickness was
brought on by the anger of gods or goddesses.
He would observe a patient's symptoms, keep
records of them and compare them with other
patients' records. He recognized the importance of taking care of the body with good
nutrition, rest and fresh air.

Hippocrates is remembered as the Greek
who introduced a scientific attitude to medicine; he made many observations about illness
and health that are still valid. He is remembered even more for the code of ethics he
practiced and passed on to physicians of today. He is considered the founder of modern
medicine.   D. H. J.

SEE ALSO: MEDICINE

Hippopotamus The hippopotamus is
sometimes called *river horse* because it
is in the horse family and lives in the
streams of tropical Africa. A male, or
bull, weighs about 4 tons (3.63 metric
tons); a female, or cow, weighs less.
They have small ears, bulging eyes,
large rounded muzzles, short tails, and
four-toed hooves.

Like all mammals they have hair, mostly
on the inside of the ears and on the muzzle
and tail. The hoof is a primitive kind in
which all four toes reach the ground. Since
the toes are even in number, they belong to
the order ARTIODACTYLA.

Front teeth *incisors* are horizontal or
tusklike, adapted for rooting up aquatic
plants. The stomach is huge and poorly
divided into sections. They are not cud
chewers. Their huge lungs let them remain
submerged for about five minutes. Eyes, on
the top of their heads, are adapted for
underwater vision.

They live in herds of about 15, basking in
the sun or in the deeper parts of the rivers
during the day. At night they come ashore,
but never travel very far from water.

Young or calves are born singly after a
gestation period of 240 days. Like all mammals, the young feed on milk. They suckle
underwater.   J.C.K.

SEE ALSO: AFRICA

Histogram A histogram is a type of
bar graph. It provides a picture of a set
of data.

Each category or class interval is represented by a portion of one axis. The frequency of each category or class interval is
represented by a bar. In the illustration
below the category is flavor of ice cream.
The bar above vanilla shows that 200 vanilla
cones were sold.   M.M.L.

ICE CREAM CONES
SOLD IN JUNE

Histology (his-TAHL-uh-jee) Histology is a study of the tissues which make up the body. A tissue is a group of cells which are alike, working together to do a definite kind of work for the body. Although all living things are composed of or made of cells, all of the cells are not alike. They become changed in ways which help them to do their work well.

The change from a simple to more complex kind of cell is known as *specialization*. The cells are known as *specialized cells*. Within the animal body there are muscle, nerve, gland, and blood cells plus many others. Because these are specialized cells they differ in appearance. However, they all come from or are developed from a more simple type of cell.

Tissues are usually combined into *organs,* where they are often arranged in layers. The stomach, HEART, and LIVER are organs.

Most organs have one or more definite functions. The function of the stomach is to do part of the work of changing the food eaten into chemicals needed to nourish or feed the body cells. The liver has more than one function. It makes or secretes *bile,* which helps in the digestion or breakdown of food. The liver also removes some of the sugar (glucose) from the blood and changes it into a form (glycogen) which can be stored for later use.

COMMON KINDS OF TISSUE FOUND
IN THE BODY

Epithelial tissues cover body surfaces and line organ cavities. There are three types or kinds of epithelia, distinguished by the shapes of the cells in the tissue. The cells of *squamous epithelium* are flat and scale-like. The cells lining the cavities of blood vessels are squamous cells. In *cuboidal* epithelium, found in the ducts of many glands, the cells are cube-shaped like a lump of sugar. *Columnar* epithelium consists of tall, rectangular cells. It occurs in the lining of the digestive tract. These three types often occur in layers and each layer may be composed of a different type.

Sustentative tissues hold together and support organs and organ systems. These tissues consist of cells and a noncellular material which surrounds the cells, called the *matrix*. Fibrous connective tissue has a matrix consisting of fibers. The fibers are of two types: *white fibers* and *elastic fibers*.

In tendons, where strength and pliability are necessary, one finds white fibers. In arteries, which stretch and vary in size, there are many elastic fibers. *Reticular connective tissue* is a framework of connective tissue cells. Inside this framework are packed cells of another type. In cartilage and bone the matrix has become hardened by the addition of calcium salts so that it is much more rigid. *Adipose tissue* ("fat") is a type of connective tissue having no matrix. The fatty materials are contained inside the adipose cell.

Muscle tissue is specialized for producing movement. Muscle cells or fibers contract and become shorter, or relax so that they become longer. Contracting *fibrils* (*myofibrils*) occur in the cytoplasm (sarcoplasm). *Smooth* muscles occur in many places in the body, such as in the walls of the digestive tract. They are long spindle shaped cells with the nucleus in the widest part of the cell. Elastic fibers around and between the cells bind them into bundles.

Attached to the skeleton are *striped* or *striated* muscles enclosed in a thick *fibroelastic* sheath. The muscles of arms and legs are examples. The muscle cells are long unbranched fibers, each containing more than one nucleus usually located just beneath the cell membrane. Bands or disks crossing the fibers give them their name.

Heart muscle is also striped, but the fibers form a branching network. They usually have several nuclei which are centrally located. Fibrous connective tissue is found between these fibers.

Nervous tissue is specialized for conducting electrochemical impulses from the place of stimulation to the cells or tissues which will respond. The body of a NERVE CELL, or *neuron*, has a set of processes called *dendrites* conducting impulses to the cell body. Another process, the *axon,* conducts them away. Axons often have a sheath of *myelin*. The axon plus its sheath is a *nerve fiber*. Neurons are arranged in chains. The point of contact between the end of the axon of one neuron and the dendrites of the next

MAIN TISSUES OF THE BODY

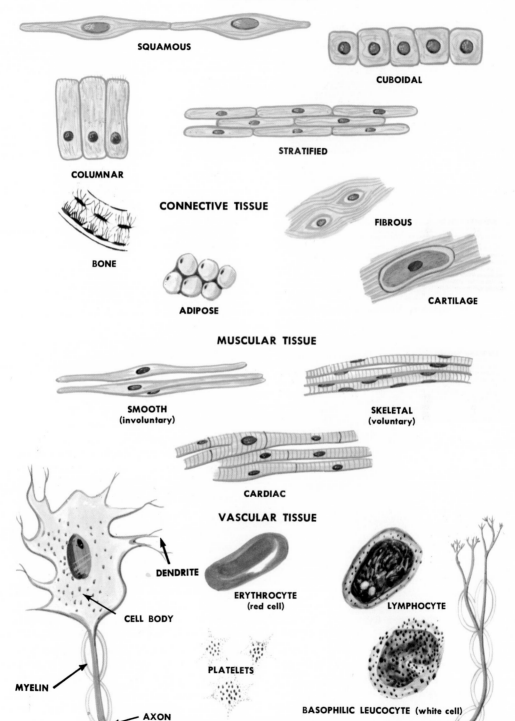

EPITHELIAL TISSUE

SQUAMOUS

CUBOIDAL

COLUMNAR

STRATIFIED

CONNECTIVE TISSUE

BONE

ADIPOSE

FIBROUS

CARTILAGE

MUSCULAR TISSUE

SMOOTH
(involuntary)

SKELETAL
(voluntary)

CARDIAC

VASCULAR TISSUE

DENDRITE

CELL BODY

ERYTHROCYTE
(red cell)

LYMPHOCYTE

PLATELETS

MYELIN

AXON

BASOPHILIC LEUCOCYTE (white cell)

NERVOUS TISSUE

✳ THINGS TO DO

HOW TO MAKE YOUR OWN TISSUE SLIDES .

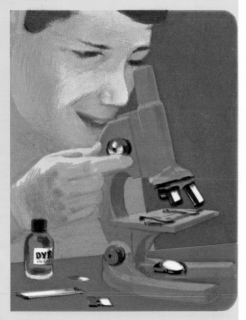

Materials: a microscope, glass slides, cover glasses, a sharp knife or razor blade, a variety of dyes—methylene blue, eosin, and crystal violet dyes are easily obtainable. (One can use red and blue ink if it is filtered first.)

1 Animal tissue may be cut from a fresh fish. With a sharp razor, slice as thin a section as possible from different organs. Observe cells from glands, tendons, epidermis, muscle, intestine, blood vessel and brain.

2 Tissue slides of plants may be made by cutting thin sections from roots, stems, leaves, fruits, flowers, and seeds. Cellular samples from the lower plant groups may be prepared in the same manner.

3 Place tissue specimen on a slide. Add a drop of dye. Blot it carefully to remove excess solution. Now put a drop of distilled water on the tissue and cover with a glass slip.

4 Observe your specimen in a microscope under low power first and then swing to high power for more detailed observation.

neuron in the chain is called the *synapse*. Electrochemical impulses can be transmitted through the synapse in only one direction, from axon to the dendrite. A nerve is made up of bundles of neurons that are surrounded by fibrous tissue.

BLOOD tissue is composed of red cells, white cells, platelets, and a liquid called *plasma*. Blood tissue serves as the transportation system of the body. In man the disk-like red blood cells (*erythrocytes*) lack nuclei and contain the protein hemoglobin. When blood circulates through the lungs, hemoglobin combines loosely with oxygen, which later is released and used by the cells. The plasma carries dissolved food products in the arteries and dissolved waste in the veins. There are several types of white blood cells (*leucocytes*). They devour (*phagocytose*) bacteria and help keep the body free from disease. *Platelets* are small bodies concerned with blood clotting.

TISSUES OF SOME COMMON ORGAN SYSTEMS

An organ system consists of a group of organs cooperating in the performance of one general function.

In the DIGESTIVE SYSTEM, the walls throughout the whole digestive tract are similar in plan and are composed of several coats or layers of tissues. The inner coat is called the *mucosa* and consists of an epithelial lining resting upon a basement membrane and of a thin layer of fibrous tissue. Next is a thin double layer of smooth muscle. Following the muscle layer is the *submucosa,* a fibrous tissue layer rich in nerve endings and blood vessels. The fourth and outer layer of the wall is known as the *external muscular* layer. It is composed of a band of muscles going around the digestive tract and a layer of muscles running lengthwise.

In different parts of the digestive tract the layers may increase or decrease in thickness. For instance, in the stomach the external muscle layer is thickened by the addition of a layer of oblique muscles, while in the rectum the longitudinal muscle layer becomes thin. The mucosa of the esophagus is arranged in longitudinal folds and contains many mucous glands. In the stomach the mucosa and submucosa are thickened by the presence of many tubular gastric glands. The surface of the mucosa in the small intestine is not only folded but bears finger-like projections known as *villi*. These increase the amount of surface in the intestine and thus aid in the process of absorbing digested food.

Arteries have three tissue layers in their walls. The types of tissue found in these layers depend on the size of the artery. The smallest vessels, the *capillaries,* consist of a single layer of flat *squamous endothelial* cells. These cells are similar to epithelial cells but have another name because they have a different origin during development. As capillaries become larger, they add to their walls layers of fibrous tissue and smooth muscle. The largest arteries consist of an inner coat of endothelium and fibrous tissue separated from a thick middle coat of elastic fibers by a tough elastic membrane. The outer layer (*adventitia*) contains white fibers, elastic fibers, and smooth muscle. In medium-sized arteries the elastic membrane is thin and wavy, and the middle layer has more smooth muscles than elastic fibers.

Veins have much thinner walls than arteries, lack elastic membranes, and the three coats are often difficult to see. Unlike arteries, veins usually contain valves which are formed from the endothelium. These open toward the heart to prevent the backward flow of blood.

Lymph vessels are like veins but have thinner walls and more valves.

In the RESPIRATORY SYSTEM, the mucosa of the tracheal tubes consists of an inner epithelium containing many mucous-secreting goblet cells covered with tiny hairlike *cilia.* The epithelium is followed by a fibrous submucosa in which are embedded cartilage rings surrounded by a small amount of muscle. The trachea branches into two tubes, *bronchi,* similar in construction to the trachea. As the bronchi branch and rebranch into smaller and smaller tubes (*bronchioles*), histological changes appear. The cartilage rings change to flat plates which continue to decrease in size until no cartilage is found in the smallest branchioles. The amount of muscle tissue associated with the rings increases as the amount of cartilage decreases. Thus smaller bronchioles generally have a ring of muscular tissue beneath the mucosa. There is much disagreement among scientists about the nature of the walls of the microscopic alveoli of the lungs.

The gland system in man is very complex. Some glands called *exocrine* glands empty or discharge their secretions through ducts. Others, *endocrine* glands, have no ducts and their secretions are put directly into the blood. Some glands discharge their secretions both ways. An example of an exocrine gland is the mammary. An example of an endocrine is the THYROID, and a gland that is both is the PANCREAS. Each gland has its own individual tissue arrangement, which is often complex.

The SKIN is composed of an outer layer of stratified squamous epithelial cells, the *epidermis,* and an underlying one of connective tissue, the *dermis*. These are separated by a fine network of reticular fibers. As the epidermis wears away it is renewed by division of the cells at the base of the layer. Many hairs, and ducts of sweat or oil glands break through the epidermis and open to the outside.

In the dermis, interlacing bundles of fibrous tissue push up into the epidermis. Coiled bases of sweat glands, hair roots, nerves, blood, and lymph vessels all occur deep in the dermis.   J. C. K.

SEE ALSO: ARTERY, CARTILAGE, CONNECTIVE TISSUE, ENDOCRINE GLANDS, EPITHELIAL TISSUE, FIBROUS TISSUE, LYMPHATIC SYSTEM, METABOLISM, MITOSIS AND MEIOSIS, MUSCLE TISSUE, SKIN MODIFICATIONS, VEIN

Hive see Bee

Hives Hives are swellings in the skin. They may be as small as a pinhead, or as large as a silver dollar. If they are on the surface of the skin, they are red and itchy. Hives inside the muscles, joints, tongue, throat, or other parts of the body are painful but do not itch. An attack of hives may happen only once or twice and never again, or it may become a chronic condition. Hives, or *urticaria,* may last several hours, a day or two, or even go on for years. They may be caused by a sensitivity to some foods, drugs, body poisons, or bacteria. In some cases the cause is not yet known.

SEE: ALLERGY

Hog see Pig

Courtesy Society For Visual Education, Inc.
Mountain holly

Holly Holly may be a low shrub or small tree 9 feet (2.7 meters) tall or even taller. The prickly-edged leaves are glossy. The many fruits are red or black.

Certain kinds of holly need the male and female trees planted near each other to insure pollination. A plant hormone is now available, however, that will force fruit to grow. The fruit is classed as a drupe, for it contains two to four little stonelike seeds. The plant grows best in acid soil.

Particular pruning and shaping will cause this plant to grow into interesting designs. This should be done during the resting period since flower buds are on the most recent stem growth.   H.J.C.

Hollyhock FLOWERS on the stalk of this plant bloom from the bottom up. They may be white, pink, yellow, salmon, or maroon. They appear from July to September. LEAVES are simple and alternate on the stiff, erect stem. The FRUIT is a dry capsule.

Hollyhocks are annuals, biennials, or perennials. Height varies from less than 2 feet to over 10 feet (.6 to 3 meters). The stem and leaf are often hairy. Leaves have serrated edges and palmate venation. Each flower has five petals and sepals, unless it is a doubled variety. These form on a terminal spike or inflorescence.

Hollyhocks belong to the mallow or Malvaceae family. Their most common disease is a rust fungus on the underside of leaves.   H.J.C.

Hollyhocks originally came from China. Many ornate hybrids may be grown today
Courtesy Society For Visual Education, Inc.

Holmium (HOLE-me-um) Holmium is a chemical element. It is a METAL of a silver-gray color. Holmium occurs in widely separated places not easy to find in the earth. It is always in combination with other ELEMENTS. It belongs to a family of elements called the *rare earths*.

Holmium was discovered in 1879. Its chemical symbol is Ho and its atomic number is 67. It is a hard metal and a good conductor of heat and electricity. It forms alloys with common metals. Its crystal structure at room temperature is hexagonal. It melts at 1500°C. and boils at 2600°C. Like all rare earths, it has three valence electrons. It forms yellow salts and pale-green oxides. The atomic weight of holmium is 164.93. SEE ALSO: ATOM, ELEMENTS   H. W. M.

Hologram (HOLE-oh-gram) A hologram is a photograph. It gives a three-dimensional view of the object photographed. The word is derived from Greek. *Holo* means whole, and *gram* means message.

A photograph is produced in a CAMERA when light reflected from an object is focused on a film. A hologram is produced on a film by two light sources. A larger beam of light is split into two parts. Part of the larger beam of light goes to the film. The light from the second part of the beam goes to the object and is then reflected to the film plate.   A.J.H.

Homeostasis (hoh-mee-oh-STAY-siss) The living body has many problems to solve in order to stay alive. It must protect itself from dangers in the outside world. It must also keep its inside parts in good working order. When danger strikes at one point, it must use the rest of its power to fight off the danger. The constant struggle to keep things running smoothly in a steady state is called *homeostasis*.

EQUILIBRIUM is another word used to describe this steady state.

One-celled plants and animals that live in salt water have the easiest time of maintaining homeostasis. The protoplasm of the CELL is quite like salt water in its salt content. Therefore, these organisms do not have too much trouble in keeping the correct amount of water in the cell. However, because the cell carries on work inside the protoplasm, it accumulates wastes which must be removed. It also needs to take in raw materials to carry on its work. The cell membrane is the structure that makes this exchange possible. It encloses the cell and allows only certain substances to pass in or out of the cell. It safeguards the equilibrium of the cell.

In more advanced plants that live on land, the loss of water from the thin leaves by EVAPORATION is a constant danger to the plant. This is why plants are so dependent on the water supply. A mechanism that helps to solve this problem is seen in the STOMATA, the tiny openings found in leaves. When the cells are full of water, the stomata open. This allows oxygen to enter the leaf and allows carbon dioxide to escape. Respiration and PHOTOSYNTHESIS can then go ahead at top speed, making food for the plant. However, a great deal of water is also lost by evaporation from these open pores. When the plant has lost too much water, the stomata close. This helps the plant to save water and return to equilibrium.

In the human body, there are complex and elegant systems to maintain homeostasis. The highly-developed NERVOUS SYSTEM is alert to the outside world as well as to conditions inside the body. A chemical system of regulation is also present—the ENDOCRINE GLANDS. These circulate hormones through the blood to every part of the body. The great success in preserving homeostasis accounts for the success of man as a living organism.   B. B. G.

SEE ALSO: LEAVES, STRESS, TRANSPIRATION

Homo sapiens (HOH-moh SAY-pee-unz) *Homo sapiens* is the scientific name for modern man, the only living species of the genus *Homo*. *Homo sapiens* is distinguished from such extinct species as *Homo Neanderthalensis* (Neanderthal man).

SEE: EVOLUTION OF MAN, HUMAN BEING

Homogeneous Homogeneous means having many parts or components that are similar or belonging to the same type. A table salt solution is a homogeneous fluid. It contains only salt in water.

Homogenization (hoh-MAHJ-uhn-ih-ZAY-shun) Homogenization is a process of mixing substances. The individual parts are broken up and mixed so completely that they usually will not separate. Homogenized MILK has the butterfat mixed with the thinner liquids.

Honey see Bee

Honeydew melon see Melon

Honeysuckle Honeysuckle may be a bush, shrub, climbing vine, or low tree. It grows up to 20 feet (6.1 meters) high. The wood is rather soft and the bark is papery. LEAVES are simple and opposite. Many kinds of honeysuckle are evergreen.

Showy, fragrant FLOWERS are perfect, having both male and female structures. Colors range from lavender, purple, yellow, orange, and pink to white. Flowers mature into berries. This FRUIT is often red but in some species it is orange, blue, purple, or black.

Sweet nectar forms at the base of the tubular corolla. Cross-pollination occurs as insects and birds are drawn to it. Bush honeysuckle attracts bees. Coral honeysuckle is pollinated by the tiny hummingbird. Japanese honeysuckle is pollinated by the sphinx moth. They are all members of the family Caprifoliacae.   H. J. C.

Honeysuckle

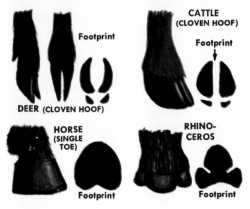

CATTLE (CLOVEN HOOF)

Footprint

Footprint

DEER (CLOVEN HOOF)

HORSE (SINGLE TOE)

RHINO-CEROS

Footprint

Footprint

Hoof Most mammals have protective coverings, such as nails or claws, at the end of arms and legs. On cows, horses, deer, sheep and the like, these coverings are called *hoofs*. The hoof is made of the same hard material as cattle horns. Hoofs do not have veins or nerves, nor do they conduct heat or cold well, so animals do not feel pain in hoofs.

During evolution, each animal's hoofs changed to meet the needs of its habits and environment. The hoofs are as healthy as the whole animal. Man's animals often have hoofs shod with metal shoes to protect them from cement.

The hoof is formed of the same keratin, a protein, that is found in horns, nails and similar appendages. Hoofs are formed by the epidermal cells as are human toenails.

Animals that have hoofs are called *ungulates,* from the Latin word *ungula,* meaning "hoof." Some are *odd-toed,* such as the horse with one toe and rhinoceros with three; others are *even-toed,* such as the pig with four toes.

In addition to protecting the soft tissue above the hoofs in normal activity, animals may use their hard hoofs as weapons. H.J.C.
SEE ALSO: ARTIODACTYLA, DEER FAMILY

Hoof and mouth disease see Animal diseases

Hooke, Robert (1635-1703) Robert Hooke was a great English experimental physicist. He constructed the first Gregorian telescope—a special kind of reflecting telescope—in 1674. In 1684 he worked out a method of telegraphy.

In 1678, Hooke announced his law of ELASTICITY, now known as *Hooke's Law*. This law states that the degree to which an elastic body stretches is in direct proportion to the force acting upon it. If the body is stretched beyond its elastic limit, its shape is permanently changed.

Born on the Isle of Wight, just off the south-central coast of England, Hooke was educated at Oxford University. He became Director of Experiments for the Royal Society of London. He helped Robert Boyle create his first successful air pump.

Although Hooke had many original ideas, he carried only a few to successful completion. He partly anticipated Newton's law of gravity and argued with him over who did it first. Though honored by his fellow scientists, Hooke had a difficult time working with many of them. He argued bitterly over scientific questions and refused to compromise or amend his own thinking. The latter part of his life was spent in embittered solitude. D. H. J.

Hookworm Hookworms are small roundworms that live in the intestines of man and other animals. They attach themselves by platelike teeth and suck blood from the intestine.

The female produces thousands of eggs daily. Eggs pass out with waste material. In moist soil they hatch into small larvae that bore into bare feet. By way of the bloodstream, these reach the intestine. Infestation is common in the southern United States.
SEE ALSO: NEMATHELMINTHES, PARASITE

Hop Hop is a perennial climbing vine of the *nettle* family. When ripe, the cone-shaped female flowers produce a yellow powder used in brewing. The Japanese hop is a decorative vine.

The hop plant is native to northern Europe and Asia. The leaves are large and have three to five lobes. The underground stem is a RHIZOME. It extends long runners. These can be cut into sections and used for propagating new plants. The female flower develops into an *achene* having one seed. Tannin, resin and oil are extracted from hops. H. J. C.

Horehound has whitish leaves and flowers

Horehound The Latin name for horehound, or hoarhound, is *Marrubium*. It refers to the bitter taste of this perennial herb of the mint family. Juices from the white flowers and woolly leaves are used for candy flavoring and in making cough medicine.

Hormone A hormone is a substance formed in certain glands and in the placenta. It is carried by the blood and tissue fluids to another organ or tissues where it stimulates or inhibits or coordinates a vital process. INSULIN is a hormone secreted by the pancreas. SEE: ENDOCRINE GLANDS, SECRETION

Hormones, plant Hormones are chemical messengers that migrate inside a plant causing things to happen. They are secreted in small amounts yet can cause a big change in the growth and development of roots, stems, leaves, flowers, or fruits.

Auxins are hormones that speed stem growth but slow root elongation. They cause a plant to bend toward light, for the auxins move to the shaded side. Cell elongation on that side makes the stem tilt toward the sunny window.

Gibberellins cause dwarf species to grow tall. They stimulate the development of fruit from unfertilized eggs. This process is called *parthenocarpy*.

Cytokinins promote production of CHLOROPHYLL. Some seeds, such as lettuce, need light to germinate. If they are treated with cytokinins, they germinate in the dark.

Ethylene is a hormone that causes fruit to ripen, chlorophyll to fade, flowers to die, and leaves to fall. People used to ripen fruit in rooms that were heated by a kerosene stove or incense pots. They thought the heat caused the ripening process. Today we know it was ethylene gas, which was a pro-

On the left is a normal geranium plant. The plant on the right is larger because it has been treated with the plant-growth hormone, gibberellic acid. The left-hand branch of the middle plant was treated, but the right branch was not and so is smaller

duct of incomplete combustion of the burning fuel. Plants produce small amounts of ethylene.

The length of daylight hours affects the flowering of a variety of plants. For years people thought that a hormone must be involved. Tentatively it has been named *florigen*. This flower-inducing hormone has not yet been isolated and extracted.

F.W. Went, in 1928, was the first scientist to isolate plant hormones. Man is now manufacturing plant hormones in laboratories. These synthetics function in the same manner as those made naturally.   H.J.C.

Horn Horn is the material found in the fingernails, claws, beaks, shells, and the like in animals. Horn is usually very hard and serves to protect

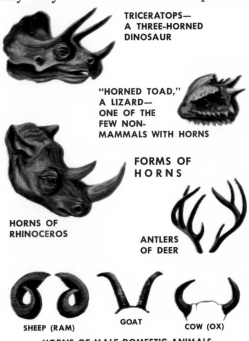

TRICERATOPS—
A THREE-HORNED
DINOSAUR

"HORNED TOAD,"
A LIZARD—
ONE OF THE
FEW NON-
MAMMALS WITH HORNS

FORMS OF
HORNS

HORNS OF
RHINOCEROS

ANTLERS
OF DEER

SHEEP (RAM)   GOAT   COW (OX)

HORNS OF MALE DOMESTIC ANIMALS

the more tender body parts.

Horn is formed by the epidermal cells and contains an albumin protein called *keratin.* Horn is found in a variety of forms such as the shell of a tortoise, hoof of a horse, or horn of a rhinoceros, which is actually a molded cluster of keratin fibers.

Horn differs not only in anatomical form but also in use as a result of environment and need of the animal. Horn has been used commercially in combs, buttons, handles and in various primitive tools. To animals, however, horn provides the appendages and coverings that enable them to live safely in their natural environment.   H. J. C.

Horns Horns are the projections on the heads of hoofed animals. They are weapons of defense.

The horns of a deer are not made of horn but are extensions of bone structure. Cattle horns have bone cores and thus when removed are hollow. They can be used for powder containers or horns to produce a musical note.   H. J. C.

Hornblende see Rocks

Horned toad see Lizard

Hornet see Wasp

Horoscope see Astrology

Horse All horses celebrate their birthdays on January first. A horse is considered a year old on the January first after it was born. It is then called a *yearling.* Until a horse is a year old, it is called a *foal.* In twelve months a young horse has grown to half its full size, but it is not full grown until it is five years old.

A female horse is called a *mare.* A male horse that can be used in breeding is a *stallion.* A young stallion is a *colt* and a young mare is a *filly.* A *gelding* is a male horse that has been castrated and cannot be used for breeding.

A mare usually starts having foals when it is four. The average mare has five or six young ones in its lifetime. The GESTATION PERIOD is eleven months.

The height of a horse is measured in hands. A hand is four inches (10.2 centimeters), and horses are measured from the ground to the highest point of the *withers,* which is the ridge between the shoulder bones. The smallest horse, a *Shetland pony,* is about ten hands high. Some horses are seventeen hands high, or five feet, eight inches (1.73 meters).

The horse sheds its thick coat of hair every spring. It can see forward, sideways, and even backwards because its eyes are at the sides of its head. A horse is easily frightened because its hearing and sense of smell are so well developed that it knows something is near before it can see what it is.

Horses that have been bred for speed have long narrow bodies, while horses that have been bred for strength have thick muscular bodies and large feet to give them good footing when pulling a heavy load.

Fifty million years ago there were horses on the plains of the western United States.

Palomino   **Hackney**   **Shire**

Horse chestnuts bear bitter, inedible nuts

They were only as big as a fox and they had toes instead of hoofs. Through the ages larger species with hoofs were developed. Those first fox-like horses disappeared from North America.

The Indians of North America had never seen a horse until the Spaniards under Hernando Cortez came to Mexico in 1519. The "wild horses" of the Western plains were probably descendants of the horses belonging to those early explorers.

Man had tamed and used horses for centuries. The early Greeks and Romans rode fast horses. Knights in armor rode them to war. The horses were strong, for the armored suits weighed as much as 400 pounds (181.4 kilograms) and often the horses wore suits of armor, too.

The Arabian horse is the oldest modern breed. Wild asses and zebras are true wild horses. They are small and not well shaped, but they can get along under difficult living conditions. Today the horse is usually used for pleasure riding and racing. On large cattle ranches of the West, horses are still needed to herd cattle.

Modern horses must be given proper care and fed properly. A horse eats oats, which are easily digested and contain valuable food elements. Horses need salt and should be given water several times daily. They like to eat grass in a pasture. A horse should be rubbed and brushed, or groomed, to remove dirt from its hair and skin.

A horse's feet follow a regular pattern when it moves; this is called a *gait*. The *walk* is a slow gait. The *trot* is a faster two-beat gait. *Canter* is an easy gallop, in rhythm. In the running walk, the horse nods its head with the hoof beats.   P.G.B.

SEE ALSO: ARTIODACTYLA, EVOLUTION

Standard-bred racing horse

Horse chestnut This tree may be 20 to 90 feet (6.1 to 27.4 meters) tall. Each leaf is made of seven leaflets, sometimes five or nine. They are arranged as the spokes in a wheel. The FLOWERS bloom in June and grow in clusters. They may be white, yellow, or greenish to shades of red.

Palmately compound LEAVES are opposite. They develop from large, sticky terminal buds which are most conspicuous in the winter. Each five-petaled flower of the inflorescence forms a panicle. This is a flower stalk with branches which, in turn, have more branches. Each bloom, when fertilized, matures into a green, thorny-coated fruit. It is a three-celled pod containing large seeds in brown nuts.

Horse chestnut belongs to the Sapindaceae family. Leaves are damaged by fungi and the larva of the tussock moth.   H. J. C.

Horse latitudes The horse latitudes are regions on the earth that are famous for calm weather and lack of wind. There is very little rainfall in these areas that have almost cloudless weather. Sailors from early America to the West Indies were often delayed for many weeks in the horse latitudes as there were no winds to fill the sails and move their ships.

The horse latitudes lie between the belts of the TRADE WINDS and the prevailing WESTERLIES at latitudes of 30° N and 30° S. They get their unusual weather from descending currents of air.   J. D. B.

SEE ALSO: EARTH, JET STREAMS, WEATHER

Example of one horsepower: one horse lifting a 550-pound weight one foot in one second

The common horsetail
Courtesy Society For
Visual Education, Inc.

Horsepower When the Scottish scientist Watt developed the steam engine, he had to compare the ability of the engine to move water from a coal mine with the ability of the horse to do the same job. Working an eight-hour day, a horse would average so much work in a second or in a minute. The time rate at which the horse worked was called the horsepower.

A strong person will do more work in a shorter time than a weaker one. The stronger worker is more powerful. In science, power is equal to work per unit time.

The average horse can work at the rate of 550 foot-pounds per second (one standard horsepower). This means that it can pull with a force of 275 pounds two feet in one second or any combination of force, distance and time to make 550 foot-pounds per second.

For example, if 55,000 foot-pounds of work is done in 5 seconds, the power rating is 55,000 divided by 5 seconds, or 11,000 foot-pounds per second. The horsepower is then 11,000 foot-pounds per second divided by 550 foot-pounds per second, or 20. (11,000 ÷ 550 = 20)

Small electric motors are called "fractional horsepower motors" because their power ratings are in fractions of one horsepower. Powerful engines often exceed 10,000 horsepower. Combinations of rocket motors can produce hundreds of thousands of horsepower.

Horsepower can be measured directly by coupling a friction device, called a Prony brake, to the output shaft of an engine or motor. This output power is known as brake horsepower. One horsepower is equal to 746 WATTS.   M.B.C.

SEE ALSO: ENGINE, FOOT-POUND, MOTOR

Horsetail About 25 kinds of this plant grow in the world today. Millions of years ago, they were plentiful and very large. Now horsetails average 5 feet (1.5 meters) high, with the range from a few inches or centimeters to 25 feet (7.6 meters) high. They thrive in wet soil or in shallow water. They grow in open meadows, in woods, in thickets, and on railroad embankments. They are called "scouring rushes" because their cell walls contain silica.

Fertilization occurs during a rain. During the Devonian period in the Paleozoic era giant horsetails contributed to the formation of coal. Horsetails belong in the group Sphenophyta under the division TRACHEOPHYTA. They are related to club moss and ferns.   H.J.C.

SEE ALSO: SPORE FORMATION

Horticulture People who study the science of growing VEGETABLES, FRUITS, and FLOWERS are called horticulturists. They learn about soil types, the needs of each kind of plant, and ways to produce new species. They must keep abreast of the latest advances in genetics, types of insecticides, methods of disease prevention, along with the variety of new machines for crop cultivation.

Horticulture is a branch of AGRICULTURE. It is now a real science. It, too, may be divided into areas of specializations. Floriculturists, fruit growers, truck farmers, and landscape artists are

New wheat strains with higher protein content are a product of the science of horticulture.

all people who work in one aspect of horticulture.

Research in the art of growing flowers has taken many directions. Floriculturists experiment to produce larger blooms and species more resistant to disease, drought, and attack by insects. In Canada three years were spent selecting and testing flowering plants for Expo '67.

Scientists at the University of Wisconsin sprayed anthogens on plants to force the flowers to bloom earlier. It proved successful on about 70 varieties. The length of daylight needed for plants to flower varies. Knowing this enables horticulturists to force plants to bloom for special occasions.

In 1966 the first multicolored delphiniums were produced by using colchicine. Gamma radiation produces mutants. Flowers develop which are doubled, fringed, fused, or striped.

Fruit growers are developing products which are larger, more attractive in color, and resistant to rots and rusts. When an auxin is introduced into a plant instead of pollen, it will stimulate fruit growth without seeds. Gibberellins initiate development of a number of seedless varieties such as tomatoes, grapes, and melons. Use of gamma rays from cobalt-60 on seeds is producing hereditary characteristics significant to fruit development. Corn bears eight ears on each stalk instead of the usual one ear.

Mechanization in harvesting fruit is improving. Berry picking is now done by machines. A finger-like apparatus pulls off mature berries. The electronic eye is used in grading tomatoes. It measures the color of juice by means of a calorimeter.

Many improvements are occurring in the field of vegetable growing. Carbon dioxide is being blown into greenhouses to produce higher yields of lettuce, cabbage, and carrots. In sand dune areas organic wastes are being used as compost and producing bumper crops. Scientists are using salt water for irrigation in drought areas where fresh water is at a premium. Snap beans, beets, and spinach have quite a tolerance for it. Potatoes have been exposed to gamma rays to increase the length of time they can be stored. These are only some examples of the research presently being conducted in the science of horticulture.

H.J.C.

SEE ALSO: BREEDING, PLANTS; CITRUS FRUITS; HORMONES, PLANT; HYBRIDIZATION

A hot spring in Iceland

Hot springs Hot springs are sources of *groundwater* that have a higher temperature than that of the human body. They are generally found in areas of relatively recent *volcanic* activity.

Hot springs are of geological importance because they indicate the manner in which groundwater circulates. Not all hot springs are heated by cooling volcanic rocks. Some originate as rainwater that has been heated at great depths within the earth and gradually rises back to the surface. Hot springs are common in the United States, Iceland, and New Zealand.

P.P.S.

SEE ALSO: GEYSER

Hothouse see Greenhouse

Housefly see Fly

Huckleberry has bell-shaped blossoms

Huckleberry Huckleberry is a woody shrub belonging to the heath family. It grows wild in the eastern part of North America.

The term *huckleberry* is commonly used for *blueberry*. They belong, however, to different groups because of fruit classification. Blueberries have smaller seeds and the fleshy pulp is not as sweet.

The dicot huckleberries have flower parts in circles of five. The berry-like fruit is actually a drupe. It contains ten bony seeds.

It thrives in cool regions where the soil is acid. It is attacked by black and powdery mildews, rusts and galls. Huckleberries are not often cultivated by man.   H. J. C.

Human being A human being is the most intelligent of all animals. He can think, judge right from wrong, and has a will to choose. Man has kept records of his life for 7000 years, but he lived long before that. Some think that a primitive type of man lived a million years ago. The Cro-Magnon man is usually considered the most similar to the modern type of thinking man, or *Homo sapiens.*

There are three groups of human beings, the *Negroid,* the *Mongoloid,* and the *Caucasoid.* These groupings have only superficial differences in structure. They are alike in most ways. They have the same physical nature as all animals, but as human beings they have a spiritual nature. They may seek the abstract qualities of goodness, beauty, and truth. With these, man can serve himself and all humanity.

A human being is social. He has the power of speech and develops his own potentialities from contact with others. He does not follow an instinctive, automatic pattern of existence but is adaptable and can adjust to all environments. He can develop and use resources of other animals, plants, land, and water. All that he knows, he has

learned. He uses the wisdom of the past to enable him to live in the present and plan for the future.   J. A. D.

SEE ALSO: EVOLUTION OF MAN

Humerus see Skeleton

Humidity Humidity is the term used to describe the moisture condition of the atmosphere. The moisture in the air is in the form of water vapor. This is water in the form of gas. Meteorologists also use the terms *capacity, absolute humidity,* and *relative humidity* when talking about the atmosphere's moisture.

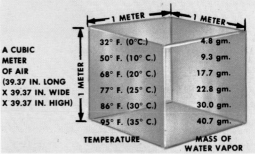

A CUBIC METER OF AIR (39.37 IN. LONG X 39.37 IN. WIDE X 39.37 IN. HIGH)

TEMPERATURE	MASS OF WATER VAPOR
32° F. (0°C.)	4.8 gm.
50° F. (10° C.)	9.3 gm.
68° F. (20° C.)	17.7 gm.
77° F. (25° C.)	22.8 gm.
86° F. (30° C.)	30.0 gm.
95° F. (35° C.)	40.7 gm.

The picture shows the amount of water in a cubic meter of air at various Fahrenheit and Celsius temperatures.

The amount of water vapor that air can hold depends almost entirely on its temperature. The amount of water vapor that air can hold at a given temperature is called *grams capacity.* Capacity may be expressed in *grams of water vapor per cubic meter,* or in *grains of water vapor per cubic foot* (common English-American measurement). There are about 400 grains in one ounce. The table shows the approximate capacity of air at various temperatures. It shows that air can hold much more water vapor when its temperature is high. It also shows that the water capacity of the air increases faster than does the temperature of the air.

Absolute humidity is the amount of water vapor actually present in the air at any given time, and is expressed in grains per cubic foot. Knowing the absolute humidity is of great importance to meteorologists in preparing forecasts.

Relative humidity is the ratio of the amount of water vapor actually in the air to the maximum amount (capacity) the air can hold at that temperature. When the air contains all the water vapor possible for it to hold at its temperature, the relative

Capacity of Air (Approximate)

Grains of Water Vapor per Cubic Foot of Air		Grams of Water Vapor per Cubic Meter of Air	
Temperature Degrees F	Water Vapor Grains per cu. ft.	Temperature Degrees C	Water Vapor Grams per cu. meter
10°	0.8	-10°	2.0
20°	1.3	-5°	3.2
30°	2.0	0°	4.8
40°	3.0	5°	7.1
50°	4.0	10°	9.3
60°	6.0	15°	13.5
70°	8.0	20°	17.7
80°	11.0	25°	22.8
90°	15.0	30°	30.0
100°	20.0	35°	40.7
		40°	51.0

humidity is 100 percent. Relative humidity is always expressed as a percent and can be defined and determined as follows: (R.H. = relative humidity; A.H. = absolute humidity; Cap. = capacity).

$$\% \text{ R.H.} = \frac{\text{A.H.}}{\text{Cap.}} \times 100$$

Let us determine the relative humidity when the absolute humidity is two grains and the air temperature is 70° F. (21.1° C.). The capacity table shows that air at 70° F. (21.1° C.) can hold eight grains. Thus,

$$\% \text{ R.H.} = \frac{\text{A.H.}}{\text{Cap.}} \times 100$$

$$= \frac{2g}{8g} \times 100 = 25\%$$

Instruments used to measure the relative humidity of the air are called HYGROMETERS. There are many different types of hygrometers, including the hair hygrometer and sling psychrometer, which measures relative humidity the most accurately.   H.S.G.

SEE ALSO: CONDENSATION, EVAPORATION, WEATHER FORECASTING

Hummingbird Hummingbirds, the smallest birds, average about 3½ inches (8.9 centimeters) long. Often mistaken for large moths, they have tubular bills with very long tongues.

Ruby-throated hummingbird

Their legs are short and their feet weak. These birds have very rapid wingbeats and they can fly backward. Thus, hummingbirds can hover over flowers while feeding.

Hummingbirds are found only in the New World. Of the 500 species, the ruby-throated hummingbird, found in the eastern United States, is the most common.

Insects, rather than nectar, form a large part of hummingbirds' food. These they catch in flowers or while flying.

They lay the smallest of bird eggs in nests perched on leaves or twigs. Two white eggs are laid and incubated for about two weeks. The young are naked when hatched but acquire down before plumage. Young are nestlings for about two weeks. Males take no part in caring for the young or in the building of the nest.   J.C.K.

Humor, aqueous and vitreous see Eye

Humus (HEW-muss) Humus is the black or brown organic part of soil which is formed by the decay (decomposition) of animal or plant matter. Humus contains chemical substances which most ground plants need.
SEE: SOIL TYPES

Hurricane Hurricanes are tropical CYCLONES. They are very large revolving storms that have high, destructive winds, heavy rains, and high waves and tides.

Many regional names are given to strong tropical cyclones (lows). Most Americans know them as *hurricanes*, a term that is used for strong tropical cyclones in the Atlantic

U.S. Air Force photo

An airplane can fly into the eye of a hurricane and test the speed of the winds and the direction in which it is moving

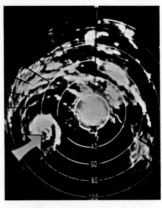

The movement of hurricanes can also be tracked by radar. Adequate warning can be given to land areas in their paths.

U.S. Air Force photo

Ocean, the Caribbean Sea, and the Gulf of Mexico. The same type of storm found in the Pacific Ocean is called a *typhoon*. Near Australia, strong tropical lows are called *willy-willies* and in the Indian Ocean, just *cyclones*. In the terminology of American meteorology, a tropical cyclone is any *closed surface* low pressure system originating in the tropics. "Closed" means that the pressure at the center of the low in the horizontal plane is lower than any other point in the system.

Tropical cyclones which affect the United States originate over the warm, tropical waters (usually above 80° F. or 26.7° C.) of the Atlantic Ocean, the Caribbean Sea, and the Gulf of Mexico. Most hurricanes develop between 5° and 15° latitude.

A hurricane has an average diameter of as much as 200 to 400 miles (322 to 644 kilometers). This very intense storm has a strange center that is a central area of descending air currents called the *eye*. Usually from 5 to 20 miles (8 to 32 kilometers) or more in diameter, this is an area of calm. The sky is clear and there is no rain.

When hurricanes hit land, they often cause great damage and may take human lives. In recent years, better systems of hurricane tracking and forecasting have been developed. People can usually be warned enough in advance to lessen the damage. In the future, people may even be able to control these storms.   H.S.G.

SEE ALSO: WEATHER, WEATHER FORECASTING, WEATHER STATION

Husbandry see Animal husbandry

Huxley, Julian Sorrell (1887-1975)

Julian Huxley is an English biologist. He is famous for his work with UNESCO, as well as for his many

books, including *Science and Social Needs, Living Thoughts of Darwin, Kingdom of the Beasts,* and *Biological Aspects of Cancer.*

Huxley is a member of a famous family. His grandfather was THOMAS HENRY HUXLEY, evolution lecturer and anatomist, and his brother is Aldous Huxley, the novelist. Sir Julian was educated at Oxford University and has taught and lectured at many colleges in England and America. He received the knighthood in 1958.   D. A. B.

Huxley, Thomas Henry (1825-1895)

Thomas Henry Huxley was a famous English naturalist. He supported the theories of evolution set forth by his friend CHARLES DARWIN.

A member of a distinguished family of English authors and scientists, Huxley was born just outside London and studied medicine at the University of London. When he was twenty years old, he enlisted in the medical service of the British Navy and spent four years sailing the Indian Ocean and the South Pacific.

During the expedition Huxley studied such sea animals as mollusks, jellyfish, and sea worms. He wrote a number of scientific papers describing the results of his investigations. These he sent back to the Royal Society in London. By the time he returned to London in 1850 his scientific reputation was well established.

Huxley retired from the navy when he was twenty-eight years old and became a lecturer on natural history at the Royal School of Mines. In 1883 he was elected president of the Royal Society, a great honor for a British scientist.   D. H. J.

Huygens, Christian (HY-guhnz)

(1629-1695) Christian Huygens was a Dutch scientist. He developed the science of OPTICS, invented the pendulum clock, and ground improved lenses for telescopes with which he made discoveries about stars and planets.

Huygens was born at The Hague, Holland, the son of Constantijn Huygens, a famous poet and scholar. His father wanted him to study law, but he preferred mathematics. This interest led him into astronomy and physics.

GALILEO had previously discovered that the swing of a PENDULUM of a given length takes the same amount of time whether the swing is a wide or narrow one. Huygens was the first to apply this principle to clocks to make them more accurate.

Huygens found a way to make the TELESCOPE larger without losing the sharpness of the image. With his improved telescope, he was the first to see the rings and one of the satellites of the planet Saturn, and to discover a nebula in the constellation Orion which still bears his name.

Scientists from the time of Aristotle onward had surmised that light might travel in waves, and they called the substance in which it was supposed to travel *ether*. Huygens was the first to develop a systematic theory to explain such wave motion. His work in this field of light and waves has been useful to physicists.   M. R. B.

SEE ALSO: LIGHT

Hyacinth

LEAVES of this flowering plant are long and slender. The stem is underground. A flower stalk ranges from 3 inches (7.6 centimeters) to 3 feet (.9 meter) high. It bears a cluster of FLOWERS.

The hyacinth bulb is a PERENNIAL herb. The grasslike LEAVES have parallel venation as do all monocots. A single flower has 3 petals, 3 sepals, and 3 carpels. There are 6 stamens to each bloom. The capsule FRUIT dehisces (opens) into 3 valves.

Spring hyacinth, 10-15 inches (25.4-38.1 centimeters) high, has blue or white funnel-shaped flowers. Musk hyacinth, 6-9 inches (15.2-22.8 centimeters) tall, has greenish-white flowers. Summer hyacinth, 36-40 inches (91.4-101.6 centimeters) tall, has bell-shaped white flowers. Small, usually blue, spring flowers of grape hyacinth are on a 3-6 inch (7.6-15.2 centimeters) stalk. All belong to the family Liliaceae.   H.J.C.

Hybridization (HY-brih-duh-ZAY-shun)

This is the process of inbreeding or crossbreeding to produce variations in living organisms. A hybrid is the result or offspring of this process. It has a combination of contrasting characteristics from two parents. Hybridization occurs naturally or is brought about by man.

In 1717, Thomas Fairchild was credited with producing the first plant hybrid made by man. In the middle 1800s GREGOR MENDEL contributed greatly to the understanding of the principles in hybridization.

A gene has a certain place or locus on a chromosome. Genes occur in pairs, each member being called an *allele*. A hybrid will show the characteristics of one or more alleles. Polyploidy is a change in the normal number of chromosomes. This is brought about

In producing hybrid corn, alternate rows of pollen stalks are either detasseled or covered

Courtesy Society For Visual Education, Inc.

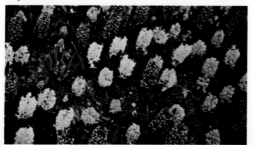

Hyacinth   Courtesy Society For Visual Education, Inc.

They will then be fertilized by another type of corn from other rows

The mule is the hybrid offspring of a horse and donkey

short and number of offspring far greater. Also, one has no problem of disposing of undesirable offspring.

In nature, hybridization may be prevented by geographic isolation, incompatibility of chromosomes, and infertility.   H. J. C.

SEE ALSO: BREEDING, HEREDITY, REPRODUCTIVE SYSTEMS

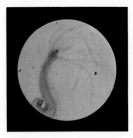

The tiny hydra may have eight thin arms. This one is magnified to 11 times life size

Photo-micrograph by National Teaching Aids, Inc.

through the use of *colchicine,* an alkaloid drug extracted from fall crocus. It prevents the spindles from forming in MITOSIS. (A cell fails to divide and ends up with more than 2 pairs of the same chromosomes.) This technique works well with plants. It produces variations and causes larger cells to form. It is not too successful in animals. Multiple sex genes too often cause sterility in hybrid animals.

Natural hybridization in plants and animals is haphazard. EVOLUTION shows many variations which occur by mutations, recombinations, and natural doubling of gene number. Introgressive hybridization was first described by Edgar Anderson. Fertile hybrids are few and they tend to cross with one of their parents. The offsprings take on more of one parent's traits than of the other's. In plant evolution this is most significant.

Hybrid vigor, or *heterosis,* is production of offspring which are better than either parent. They often have larger parts, produce more, grow faster, and have greater resistance to an adverse environment. They result from outcrossing two parents of the same or closely related species. Hybrid hogs produce more ham and bacon. When beef and dairy cattle are bred with each other the calves produce better veal. *Cattalo* is the offspring of a bull and a buffalo cow. Mating a male burro and a female horse produces a *mule.* A *liger* is the cub of an African lion and tiger. A *zonkey* is the hybrid of a jackass and a zebra mare.

In plant hybrids, melons have a higher sugar content, cotton has longer fibers, oats are resistant to smut, and grapes are seedless. Hybrids of cliff cabbage have resulted in kohlrabi, broccoli, and Brussels sprouts. Plants which can be propagated asexually make good hybrids for they keep the same traits. If it is necessary to use seeds, the recessive qualities begin to show up and the offspring become quite varied. One, then, must isolate desired traits and inbreed it to a pure strain. It is far easier and less time consuming for man to cause mutations in plants than in animals. The gestation period of plants is

Hydra Hydras are animals that are like small sacks with a number of thread-like tentacles ("arms") around the mouth. They are *coelenterates.* Most of their relatives live in the sea and include jellyfish, sea anemones, sea pens and corals.

The hydra lives in calm, fresh water, often attached to the underside of water plants. It can contract its body into a ball or stretch into a long cylinder.

For food, the hydra preys upon small crustaceans, worms and insect larvae. Batteries of several kinds of stinging cells occur on the tentacles. The stinging apparatus, a tiny coiled spine (*nematocyst*), is inside a trigger-equipped cell. When prey touches the trigger, the nematocyst discharges. Some nematocysts are barbed and secrete a paralyzing chemical. Others loop around the prey like lassos. Entrapped and paralyzed, the prey is brought to the mouth by the tentacles. Food is digested inside the sack-like body. Undigested parts are eliminated out the mouth.

Hydras reproduce asexually by forming a small bud on the body wall. The bud grows, develops mouth and tentacles, breaks off and lives an independent life. Sexual reproduction also takes place. In some species, male hydras develop *spermaries* and females develop *ovaries.* Other species are *hermaphroditic.* After fertilization, a two-layered embryo is formed. It acquires a shell, breaks loose and sinks to the pond bottom. A young hydra may hatch after a week or the embryo may winter on the bottom.   J. C. K.

SEE ALSO: COELENTERATA

✳ THINGS TO DO

HOW DOES A HYDRA ATTACK ITS FOOD?

1 These little fresh water animals may be collected from a pond or stream. Place the plants they are attached to with some of the pond water in a glass jar. Transport them back to your room for experimentation.

2 Do not feed the hydra for two days so they will be very hungry.

3 With an eye dropper, carefully suck up the hydra and place it on a glass slide. When it is relaxed and extended, gently place a daphnia (small crustacean or water flea) in front of its tentacles. Keep it moist.

4 First the hydra will strike out with its tentacles, paralyzing the daphnia with numerous stinging cells. Then the tentacles wrap around the flea and bring it into the mouth.

5 There are other experiments to do with these fascinating animals. Shine a bright light on the hydra. What is its reaction? When the hydra is fully extended, take a pencil and tap the end of its tentacles. What happens? Cut the hydra into two parts. Watch each piece regenerate.

Hydrangeas have large, colorful flowers

Hydrangea (hy-DRAYN-juh) It is a flowering shrub that grows from 2 to 15 feet (.6 to 4.6 meters) high. LEAVES are simple and opposite on the branches. Clusters of FLOWERS may be white, pink, or blue. The FRUIT is a dry capsule which is often ribbed.

Each flower of the inflorescence has 4 to 10 petals, 4 to 5 sepals, 5 or more stamens, and 2 to 10 carpels. Marginal flowers are often sterile and sometimes all of them are unable to produce seed. A pink bloom on a hydrangea will turn blue if the soil becomes acid. Peat moss and leaf mold will change an alkaline soil to acid.

Its name is given to a group of plants called the Hydrangeaceae family. Diseases of the hydrangea are caused by red spiders, leaf tyer worms, and rose chafer. Botrytis blight is an infection by a fungus.   H. J. C.
SEE ALSO: SHRUB

Hydrates Some compounds, especially salts, combine with water to form hydrates. Hydrates have a crystalline form.

Hydrates have a definite chemical composition and the amount of water present is in fixed proportions by weight. When heated, they lose the water of hydration and the chemical change results in a dry powder instead of crystals. Gypsum ($CaSO_4 \cdot 2H_2O$) is a naturally occurring hydrate. The anhydrous (without water) form is $CaSO_4$ (calcium sulfate). Washing soda, $Na_2CO_3 \cdot 10H_2O$, is a hydrate which contains 10 molecules of water.   J. H. D.
SEE ALSO: ANHYDRIDE, CRYSTAL

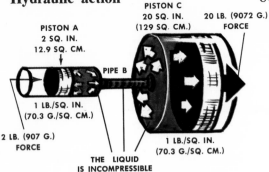

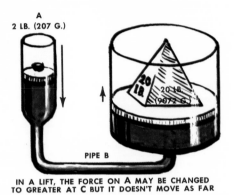

IN A LIFT, THE FORCE ON **A** MAY BE CHANGED
TO GREATER AT **C** BUT IT DOESN'T MOVE AS FAR

Hydraulic action When you turn on a faucet, water comes out. There is pressure pushing it. This is called hydraulic action. The pressure pushing the water in a faucet may come from a tank which sits on legs about 100 feet (30.5 meters) high, or from a pump in the ground. The blood in the human body circulates due to pressure supplied by the pumping action of the heart. *Liquids* when pressed form hydraulic action. Since liquid cannot be pressed or packed, when pressure is applied to a small surface of liquid, that pressure will spread throughout the liquid to all of its outer surfaces.

The actual basis of hydraulic action is explained by Pascal's Law, which states: Any change of pressure applied to the surface of a confined fluid is transmitted unchanged to all parts of the liquid. Also, the internal pressure is equal in all directions at any point in the liquid.

It can easily be seen that a large force can be obtained from a small applied force. If one supposes piston A has an area of 2 square inches (12.9 square centimeters)

and that a force of 2 pounds (907 grams) is exerted on that piston, then the pressure is 1 lb./in.^{2} (70.3 g./cm.^{2}). This pressure is then transmitted through pipe B to piston C. If piston C has an area of 20 in.^{2} (129 cm.^{2}), then the force exerted on the face would be 20 lbs. (9072 g.). Thus since the area is ten times as great, the force exerted is ten times as great. This system is called a *hydraulic jack*.   A.E.L.

Hydrocarbon This is the simplest class of *organic,* or carbon-chain, chemical compounds. These are made up of CARBON and HYDROGEN and nothing else. The carbon atoms are combined into either a closed or an open chain. The chain is surrounded by attached hydrogen atoms.

A carbon atom can unite with four hydrogen atoms to form the hydrocarbon *methane,* which is a gas. The chemical formula of methane is CH_4. The structural formula is

$$\begin{array}{c} H \\ H\!:\!\overset{\cdot\cdot}{\underset{\cdot\cdot}{C}}\!:\!H \\ H \end{array}$$

showing that each of the four outer electrons of carbon is paired with a single electron of a hydrogen atom to form four covalent bonds. One carbon atom can also unite with another carbon and six hydrogens to form the hydrocarbon *ethane,* C_2H_6 or

$$\begin{array}{c} H\ H \\ H\!:\!\overset{\cdot\cdot}{\underset{\cdot\cdot}{C}}\!:\!\overset{\cdot\cdot}{\underset{\cdot\cdot}{C}}\!:\!H \\ H\ H \end{array}$$

In this way, compounds having more and more carbon atoms can be formed. For example, *propane,* C_3H_8; or *butane,* C_4H_{10}. More complex arrangements are also possible, but the term "hydrocarbon" usually refers to a compound containing *only carbon* and *hydrogen,* with the carbon atoms arranged linearly (not in a circle), and with only single, covalent bonds between carbon atoms. Such simple hydrocarbons form what is called the *paraffin series*. The first four members of the paraffin series were just discussed. They are all gases at room temperatures. The next thirteen members of the paraffin series, C_5H_{12} to $C_{17}H_{36}$, are oily liquids. Hydrocarbons with 18 or more carbon atoms are greasy solids.   H. K. S.
SEE ALSO: CHEMISTRY, ORGANIC COMPOUNDS

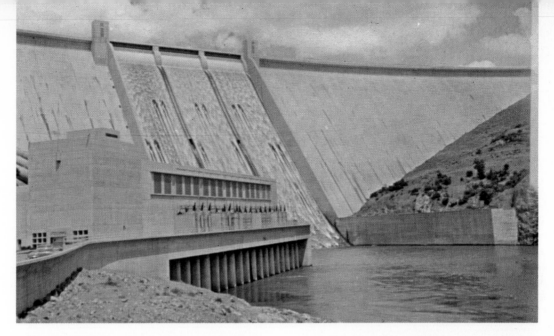

Modern dams may be equipped for the production of vast amounts of hydroelectric power

The giant turbines being installed above are very different from the old paddle wheels

All photos courtesy of Allis-Chalmers Mfg. Co.

Special cradles within which the wheels rest increase the power of the moving water

Hydrochloric acid Hydrochloric acid is one of the cheapest and one of the strongest acids. It is used in the manufacture of corn syrup, dyes, glue, and in many industrial processes.

The pure acid is the solution in water of a colorless, strong smelling, sour tasting poisonous gas, *hydrogen chloride*.

A common method of producing hydrogen chloride is by dropping concentrated SULFURIC ACID upon a metallic chloride, usually table salt. The chemical reaction may be described:

$$NaCl + H_2SO_4 \rightarrow NaHSO_4 + HCl$$

Early alchemists used this method and called the acid "marine acid air." The term "muriatic acid," from the word for brine, is still used today.   J. M. C.

SEE ALSO: ACIDS AND BASES, DIGESTIVE SYSTEM

Hydroelectric power Electricity which is generated by using the force created by flowing water is usually called *hydroelectric power*. In most cases hydroelectric power plants are installed at the base of huge DAMS where the reservoir supplies ample amounts of water to power the TURBINES.

The water from the storage reservoir of the dam is brought to the turbines through large steel pipes called *penstocks*. By the time the water has reached the turbine, it has gained a tremendous amount of MOMENTUM. As the water strikes the blades of the turbine, a device somewhat similar to a paddle wheel, it causes the turbine to rotate at a very high speed. The shaft of the turbine drives a GENERATOR which produces the electricity by shaft rotating in a mag-

865

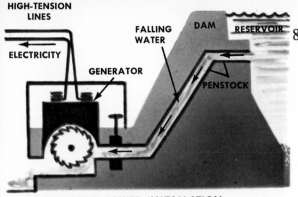

HIGH-TENSION LINES

ELECTRICITY

GENERATOR

FALLING WATER

DAM

RESERVOIR

PENSTOCK

HYDROELECTRIC POWER INSTALLATION

(SCHEMATIC)

TURBINES SUCH AS THIS CAN CHANGE 90% OF WATER'S ENERGY TO ELECTRICITY

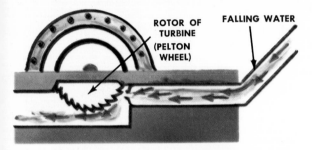

ROTOR OF TURBINE (PELTON WHEEL)

FALLING WATER

netic field. The generated electricity is taken from the generator and supplied to surrounding areas through high tension (high voltage) lines.

Most hydroelectric power installations consist of a number of turbines and generators just like a conventional steam-powered generating plant. The average hydroelectric plant can produce thousands of volts of electricity at a constant rate.

Although the principles of the operation of the turbine and generator are the same in a hydroelectric installation, the source of water is not always a dam. In many instances the natural flow of the water in a river is rapid enough so that it can be fed directly to the turbines without having to add extra energy to the flow. Also some natural WATERFALLS can be used as sources of water power for hydroelectric generators. The power plant at the base of Niagara Falls is an example of this type of installation.

There are also instances where there is sufficient water but no natural site available for a huge dam or reservoir. Here the energy is supplied to the water by pumping it into small storage reservoirs at an elevation considerably greater than the turbine itself. In essence this creates a man-made waterfall to supply energy to the water. This type of installation is very costly and is used only where no other source of electricity is readily available.   A. E. L.

SEE ALSO: DYNAMO, ELECTRICITY, WATER

Hydrogen   Hydrogen is an odorless, colorless, and tasteless GAS that is the lightest of all chemical elements. The hydrogen ATOM, which is made up of a single proton and a single electron surrounding it, is the simplest of all atoms. DEUTERIUM, a hydrogen isotope, has one proton and one neutron in each nucleus and has an atomic weight twice that of ordinary hydrogen. In *tritium,* a third isotope, the nucleus contains one proton and two neutrons. It weighs three times as much as ordinary hydrogen.

The sun and distant stars are made up largely of hydrogen and HELIUM. On earth, hydrogen is rarely found alone. It is usually combined with some other element. The human body contains hydrogen, as do other animals, plants, and many minerals. Chemicals called ACIDS AND BASES contain hydrogen. In acids it often appears as the *hydronium ion,* H_3O^+, while in bases it often occurs in the *hydroxyl ion,* OH^-.

Hydrogen does not combine with as many elements as oxygen does, and it reacts more readily with nonmetals. Its most plentiful and important combination is with oxygen to form WATER. When air or oxygen and hydrogen are combined and the mixture is ignited, an explosion occurs. Burned in air, hydrogen combines with oxygen, and water is formed as it gives off a very hot colorless flame. Unlike oxygen, hydrogen does not support life, although breathing it has no directly harmful effects.

Hydrogen can be changed to a liquid which boils at $-253°$ C $(-423.4°$ F) and to a solid which melts at $-259°$ C $(-434.2°$ F). It is easily produced by ELECTROLYSIS of water, in which electric current breaks down into its two components—oxygen and hydrogen. Passing steam over coal or coke produces hydrogen mixed with carbon monoxide or carbon dioxide. When NATURAL GAS is passed over heated brick, it produces carbon black and hydrogen.

Hydrogen atoms usually are found combined with other atoms, often with those of nonmetallic elements, such as oxygen, carbon, or sulfur.

Because it forms bonds with oxygen atoms

so strongly, hydrogen can "steal" oxygen from metallic oxides, forming water and leaving free metal behind. This is one aspect of the chemical process called *reduction*. At extreme temperatures, hydrogen protons fuse together with explosive violence. This is the principle of the *hydrogen bomb*.

In the early history of CHEMISTRY, hydrogen was often mistaken for other gases. In 1766 Henry Cavendish showed that it was an independent material that formed water when united with oxygen. LAVOISIER renamed it *hydrogen* (Greek for "water former"), which was more fitting than the name "inflammable air" given to it by JOSEPH PRIESTLEY in 1781.   D. C. H.
SEE ALSO: AIRSHIPS, ELEMENTS, HYDROLYSIS

Hydrogen bond A hydrogen bond occurs when hydrogen bonds to two atoms. It is one of the three chemical bonds. The other two are *covalent* and *ionic* bonds.

The hydrogen bond is the weakest chemical bond. It occurs when hydrogen bonds with elements such as oxygen, nitrogen, and fluorine. The electron from the hydrogen is drawn to one side, causing the molecule to be positive. This positive side of hydrogen attracts a second molecule. This is a hydrogen bond.

The hydrogen bond plays an important role in WATER chemistry. This bond also causes the *helical* structure in *nucleic acids*.

Hydrogen peroxide see Hydrogen, Oxide

Hydroid colony This colony is composed of a group of various water animals. They grow attached to something such as a rock or plant. Often they share a branched digestive cavity. The mouths of individuals are ringed with TENTACLES that capture food and carry it to the mouths where it enters the common digestive cavity.

The feeding individuals of a hydroid colony are called *polyps*. Other individuals specialize in defense. These have body cells that, when stimulated, discharge several kinds of threads called NEMATOCYSTS. Some of these are barbed and inject poison into prey. Others are sticky, entrapping prey by entanglement.

Part of the colony are reproductive polyps. Some reproduce asexually by budding off free living sexually reproducing individuals called *medusae*. On these, mouths hang down like handles and tentacles are around an umbrella-like rim. Their eggs and sperm, after fertilization, form hydroids.

The presence of several types of individuals in a colony, each with a different function, is called *polymorphism*. Hydroids are excellent examples of this.   J. C. K.
SEE ALSO: COELENTERATA

Hydrolysis (hy-DRAHL-uh-sis) Hydrolysis is the DECOMPOSITION of a chemical in the presence of water. It results in the formation of two other compounds. The water itself breaks up, and its H ion and OH ion become part of the reaction chemicals formed.

Typical hydrolysis involves a salt compound, type RX, and water, H_2O. The RX separates (ionizes) as it reacts with water:

$$RX + H_2O \rightleftharpoons ROH + HX$$

This reaction, opposite to *neutralization*, forms an *acid* (HX) and a *base* (ROH). Hydrolysis occurs, in general, when the acid and the hydroxide are weak electrolytes.

Organic hydrolysis occurs with chemicals such as starch or sugar.   D. A. B.
SEE ALSO: ELECTROLYSIS, NEUTRALIZATION

Hydrometer (hy-DRAHM-uh-ter) A hydrometer is an instrument for measuring DENSITY or *specific gravity* of liquids. Density means the weight of a given volume of a material. A hydrometer is often used to measure strength of antifreezes and acid solutions, as in automobile storage cells. Strong solutions show greater density than weaker (more dilute) solutions. The moving part of a hydrometer is a hollow glass bulb or float.

When the liquid being tested is drawn into it, the bulb sinks part of the way. The level at which it stops sinking is read on the attached scale. This number is the density of the liquid.

When a storage battery is charged by an electric current, the solution of SULFURIC ACID inside becomes more dense. As the

DO YOU NEED SOIL TO GROW CORN AND BEANS?

1 Make solution A by dissolving 2 teaspoons of calcium nitrate, ½ tsp. of potassium acid phosphate, 1¼ tsp. of Epsom salts, and ¼ tsp. of ammonium sulfate into one cup of water. Pour this solution into 2½ gallons of distilled water.

2 Make solution B by dissolving ⅛ teaspoon of each of these materials into a cup of water: zinc sulfate, manganese sulfate, and boric acid.

3 Make solution C by dissolving ⅛ tsp. of ferrous sulfate into a cup of water. Now add one teaspoon of solution B and 3 tablespoons of solution C to solution A.

4 Secure a large aquarium or similar container. Take a piece of wire mesh the same width, but several inches longer than the inside dimensions of the aquarium. Bend the ends and insert it so it forms a table a few inches above the floor of the container.

5 Pour in the mixture prepared above to the level of the wire. Scatter sphagnum moss over the wire table. This serves only to hold the seeds.

6 Place the corn and bean seeds all over the top of the moss. The seeds will germinate, roots growing down into the solution. Continue to maintain the level of the solution throughout the growing period.

7 Experiment with other plants. Can you get the fruit of a tomato plant to develop without soil?

battery is used and discharged, the solution gradually becomes less dense. A hydrometer is used to show such changes in density. When the solution is dense, the hydrometer sinks to a certain depth; then as it becomes less dense, the instrument must sink deeper to displace enough liquid to equal its own weight. The numbers on the scale tell what the condition of the battery is. A similar method is used to measure the ability of an ANTIFREEZE to protect an automobile radiator and engine water jacket from freezing.

V. V. N.

Hydrophobia see Rabies

Hydroponics (hy-druh-PAHN-icks) Hydroponics is a way of growing plants in water. No soil is needed because necessary plant foods are added to the water. Seeds are sown on a bed which is suspended over water. Sometimes plants are grown in clean gravel or sand to which food solution is added.

Soilless culture began as a laboratory technique for studying root development, plant nutrients, and the deficiencies caused by withholding necessary elements. It is useful economically since vegetables can grow in areas where there is a lack of good soil. Some off-season crops, such as tomatoes, are grown hydroponically. The quality of hydroponic crops is comparable to those grown in soil.

E.R.B.

SEE ALSO: AQUACULTURE

Hydroxide Hydroxide is the name commonly given to certain chemicals that contain HYDROGEN and OXYGEN. Acids mixed with certain hydroxides turn into salts and water. They are said to be *neutralized*.

Hydroxides are compounds having the HYDROXYL OH⁻ radical. In general, the term refers to the basic hydroxides formed from metallic elements in solution, as potassium hydroxide. Solutions of basic hydroxides make red litmus blue. Other hydroxides, when mixed with water, can be acid, amphoteric, or neutral. Alcohols contain OH group but do not act like bases.

Hydroxides have a bitter taste as is seen in soapy water which contains released hydroxyl ions. Household AMMONIA is a 3% solution of ammonium hydroxide.   J. M. C.

SEE ALSO: ACIDS AND BASES, METAL, SALTS

Hydroxyl The combination of an oxygen atom with a hydrogen atom is called the *hydroxyl ion* or the *hydroxyl group*. It forms an important part of such chemical compounds as *bases, alcohols, phenols, carboxylic acids, carbohydrates,* and many others.

The hydroxyl ion is characterized by the "extra" electron it carries, which gives it a negative electrical charge when in water solution. In this form it is called the *hydroxyl ion,* OH⁻. They are released into the water whenever any *bases* (sodium hydroxide, calcium hydroxide, ammonium hydroxide, etc.) are dissolved in it. Hydroxyl ions readily react with hydrogen ions, H_3O+ to form water according to the equation:

$$OH- + H_3O+ \rightarrow 2H_2O.$$

Since the hydroxyl ion also reacts with fats and greases, it forms good detergents.

In molecular compounds, particularly carbon-chain organic compounds, the hydroxyl group remains firmly attached to the remainder of the molecule by a *covalent* (shared electron-pair) bond. This is the case in ethyl alcohol, C_2H_5OH, phenol alcohol, C_6H_5OH, and acetic acid, CH_3CO-OH. Such compounds tend to be acids rather than bases. Solutions containing hydroxyl ion must be handled carefully, since they may strongly affect the skin.   C. F. R.

SEE ALSO: ACIDS, ALCOHOL, BASES

Chicago Natural History Museum

Striped hyena

Hyena These mammals are doglike with longer front legs than hind. Their heads are large compared to the size of their bodies, their jaws are very powerful, and their ears are pointed. They feed on dead animals. Hyenas have an odd, laughlike cry.

Due to weak-muscled hindquarters, the hyena cannot run fast enough to pursue prey. Thus they are scavengers, digging up the meat hidden or left by other animals. Strong front paws are adapted for digging. Hyenas are solitary and active at night.

There are three kinds of hyena in Africa and Asia. These are the brown, the spotted, and the striped.   J. C. K.

SEE ALSO: CARNIVORE

Hygiene (HY-jeen) Hygiene is the science that deals with the proper care of the human body and mind.

Good nutrition is important for good health. Eating too much "junk food" and not enough good food will cause disorders. Vitamins are needed for healthy skin, proper bone development, good eyesight, and normal nervous reactions. Proteins are required for building cells and repairing tissues. Minerals are essential for bone growth.

Drinking eight glasses of water a day helps dilute urine, which is highly acid and may harm the delicate kidney tissues.

False teeth are much more difficult to use than your own. Therefore, brushing regularly and using dental floss are good hygienic practices to prevent decay.

Daily exercise improves muscle tone, speeds circulation, and promotes correct posture.   H.J.C.

SEE ALSO: NUTRITION, SEWAGE DISPOSAL, TEETH, VITAMIN, VITAMIN DEFICIENCY, WATER PURIFICATION

✳ THINGS TO DO

HOW MUCH WATER VAPOR IS IN THE AIR TODAY?

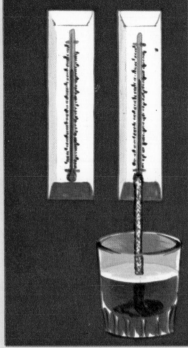

DRY BULB		TEMPERATURE DIFFERENCES BETWEEN READINGS OF WET AND DRY BULBS													
C°		.6°	1.1°	1.7°	2.2°	2.8°	3.3°	3.9°	4.4°	5.0°	5.6°	6.1°	6.7°	7.2°	7.8°
	F°	1°	2°	3°	4°	5°	6°	7°	8°	9°	10°	11°	12°	13°	14°
17.8°	64°	95	90	84	79	74	70	65	60	56	51	47	43	38	34
18.3°	65°	95	90	85	80	75	71	66	61	57	53	48	44	40	36
18.9°	66°	95	90	85	80	75	71	66	61	57	53	48	44	40	36
19.4°	67°	95	90	85	80	75	71	66	62	58	53	49	45	41	37
20°	68°	95	90	85	80	76	71	67	62	58	54	50	46	42	38
20.6°	69°	95	90	85	81	76	72	67	63	59	55	51	47	43	39
21.1°	70°	95	90	86	81	77	72	68	64	59	55	51	48	44	40
21.7°	71°	95	90	86	81	77	72	68	64	60	56	52	48	45	41
22.2°	72°	95	91	86	82	77	73	69	65	61	57	53	49	45	42
22.8°	73°	95	91	86	82	78	73	69	65	61	57	53	50	46	42
23.3°	74°	95	91	86	82	78	74	69	65	61	58	54	50	47	43
23.8°	75°	96	91	86	82	78	74	70	66	62	58	54	51	47	44
24.4°	76°	96	91	87	82	78	74	70	66	62	59	55	51	48	44
25°	77°	96	91	87	83	79	74	71	67	63	59	56	52	48	45
25.6°	78°	96	91	87	83	79	75	71	67	63	60	56	53	49	46
26.1°	79°	96	91	87	83	79	75	71	68	64	60	57	53	50	46
26.7°	80°	96	91	87	83	79	75	72	68	64	61	57	54	50	47

1 Since commercial thermometers (not fever thermometers) do not always agree, select two that are recording the same temperature in the store before you purchase them.

2 Suspend them from a support. Cut the metal ends off a shoe string.

3 Pull the opening of one end of the shoestring over the bulb of the thermometer which will be designated the wet-bulb. Place the other end of the shoestring in a glass of water.

4 To calibrate the relative humidity for any particular day, find the difference in the readings of the dry and wet bulb thermometers. With the help of the chart you will be able to find an approximate answer. For example, if the wet bulb reading is seventy degrees and the dry bulb reading is eighty degrees, the difference in the readings is ten degrees. Find the dry bulb temperature and the ten degree difference on the chart. The approximate relative humidity is seen to be fifty-five per cent in this case.

Hygrometer A hygrometer is one of several instruments used to determine the amount of moisture in the air. The *psychrometer* is the hygrometer used in almost all WEATHER STATIONS and uses the wet-dry bulb method. It consists of two identical THERMOMETERS mounted beside each other on a common base—the wet bulb being mounted a little lower than the dry bulb. The wet bulb is wrapped in muslin that is dipped in distilled water, while the dry bulb is left uncovered. The device is then whirled briskly, or a fan is directed on it. The water in the muslin evaporates and cools the bulb. The temperatures of both thermometers are then checked with tables that give the relative HUMIDITY based on their readings.

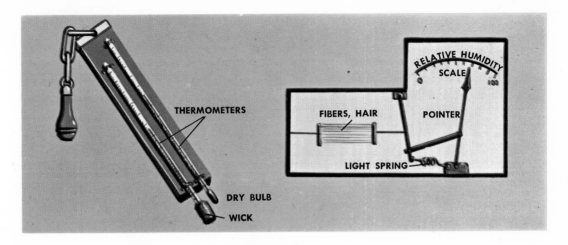

THERMOMETERS

DRY BULB

WICK

RELATIVE HUMIDITY SCALE

FIBERS, HAIR

POINTER

LIGHT SPRING

Wet bulb and direct-reading hygrometers

When this same apparatus is mounted on a table with a relative humidity scale at the bottom and then enclosed in a frame, it is called a *direct-reading* hygrometer or a *hygrodeik*.

Hair hygrometers use an organic fiber which lengthens when damp and shrinks when dry, activating a pointer which moves across a scale of per cent relative humidities. The readings are not consistent; therefore, this hygrometer is not reliable.

The *dew-point* hygrometer uses ETHER in a highly-polished cup. Evaporation of the ether is speeded when air is blown through it. When evaporation cools the cup enough, dew forms on it. A table gives the relative humidity based on the temperature of the cup at DEW POINT and the temperature of the atmosphere. In *chemical* hygrometers, moisture in a specific volume of air is absorbed by sulfuric acid or calcium chloride, and the increase in weight is relative to the amount of moisture in the air.

Hygrographs are hygrometers in which a continuous record of relative humidity is kept by a pen moving over a mechanically-operated rotating drum.   D. C. H.

Hyperopia see Farsightedness

Hypertension Hypertension is the medical name for high BLOOD PRESSURE in the arteries. Untreated, it can result in *stroke* and *heart failure.* Symptoms of hypertension include dizziness and headache. It is usually detected by measuring blood pressure.

Hypertonic solution (hy-per-TAHN-ick) A hypertonic solution is a solution with greater osmotic pressure than that of another solution which is taken as a standard. Medically, it means a fluid with a higher percentage of salts than that of the blood plasma or cells. SEE: OSMOSIS

Hypertrophy (hy-PURR-truh-fee) A callus which forms on a hand or foot is an example of hypertrophy. *Hypertrophy* means that the enlargement of the tissues of an organ is not due to cell division. Enlargement resulting from cell division is described by the word *hyperplasia*.

Both of the words *hypertrophy* and *hyperplasia* are most commonly used in the field of PATHOLOGY (the science of disease). If the valves of the heart do not function normally, hypertrophy takes place. The muscles of the heart increase in size. Following the removal of, or injury to, a kidney, hypertrophy takes place in the remaining one.

Hypertrophy and hyperplasia are normal for the pregnant uterus. During the early stages of PREGNANCY, when the embryo is small, the uterus increases in size by cell division (hyperplasia). During later stages, under the influence of complex hormones, and because of pressure from the growing embryo, the muscle cells of the uterus increase in size by hypertrophy.   J. C. K.

Hypocotyl see Seed

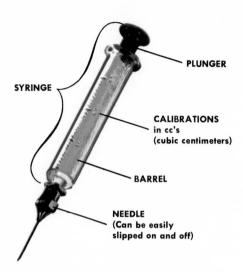

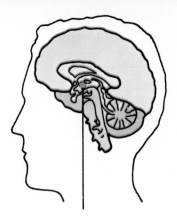

The hypothalamus lies at the base of the brain

Hypodermic syringe and needle

Hypodermic *Hypo* means "under" or "below" and *derm* means "skin." Hypodermic usually refers to a method of injecting liquid medicine under the skin with a *syringe* and *needle*.

The syringe has a barrel and plunger. Medicine is drawn into the syringe. The air is forced out by holding the syringe in an upright position and slowly pressing the plunger until all air bubbles are expelled. The skin is cleaned with a small gauze pad usually medicated with ALCOHOL. Skin is held between the forefinger and thumb. The needle is inserted, and the plunger is pulled back slightly. If blood appears in the syringe, it may mean that the needle is in a vein and a new site must be chosen. This rarely happens since a hypodermic needle is smaller and shorter than the larger needles that are used for intravenous or intramuscular injections. Following the injection, the skin is sponged with a small gauze pad.

Air guns which shoot hypodermic needles are used to capture dangerous wild animals alive and uninjured for zoos. The needles release a stunning or tranquilizing drug. M. I. L.
SEE ALSO: DRUGS

Hypotension Hypotension is the medical name for BLOOD PRESSURE that is too low. It can result from a disease or a sudden loss of blood, which is a serious emergency.

Hypothalamus (hy-po-THAL-uh-mus) The hypothalamus forms the floor of the third cavity or ventricle in the brain. Below and connected to it is the stalk of the PITUITARY GLAND. The hypothalamus helps regulate metabolism or body functioning.

In regulating some metabolic activity, the hypothalamus works through the AUTONOMIC NERVOUS SYSTEM. Anterior centers are active in slowing down heartbeat, increasing the amount of blood insulin (HORMONE of PANCREAS), and increasing urination. There are centers for control of sleep, hunger, and temperature (lowered by stimulation of sweat glands). Posterior centers have an opposite or antagonistic effect on these.

Nerve cells in the hypothalamus secrete two hormones that are stored in, and released by, the posterior pituitary lobe. One is *vaso pressin*. It acts on small arteries, raising blood pressure and increasing water reabsorption by the kidney. The other is *oxytocin*. It causes milk ejection in milk glands and uterine contraction. Hormones secreted into the blood by the hypothalamus may also control the release of other hormones in the anterior lobe.   J. C. K.
SEE ALSO: BRAIN

Hypothesis see Scientific method

Hypotonic solution (hy-poh-TAHN-ick) A hypotonic solution is a solution with lower osmotic pressure than that of another solution taken as standard. Medically, it means a fluid with a lower percentage of salts than that of blood plasma or cells.
SEE: OSMOSIS

Ibex   Ibis

Ibex The ibex is a mountain goat. It has a stocky body and long, heavy, rough horns which curve back. At one time it was close to extinction in the Swiss Alps; it is now under government protection. It also lives in herds high in the Himalayas of central Asia and in North Africa.

Ibis The ibis is a bird with long stiltlike legs, a long neck, and a long curved bill. It resembles its HERON and STORK relatives except that it flies with its neck extended and the curve of its bill is downward. It lives in swamps eating fish and crustaceans, and nesting in large colonies. The green and brown glossy ibis, white-faced glossy ibis, and white ibis are native to the subtropical United States.

Ice When a substance changes from liquid state to solid state it is said to *freeze*. Ice is merely the frozen or solid state of WATER, made up of tiny crystals, bound together to form larger pieces. Because ice is crystalline in nature, it melts at a very definite temperature, defined as 0° Centigrade or 32° Fahrenheit. The melting point of water is used as a temperature standard all over the world.

Water is also one of the very few materials which expands upon freezing. This is the reason water will break a glass jar if it is

filled and then frozen. Increased pressure will cause ice to melt at a lower temperature than it would normally. A very interesting demonstration of this is to suspend a fine wire with weights attached to each end over a block of ice. The ice directly under the wire will melt, and the water flows around it only to be refrozen. The wire will actually pass through the block, leaving it in one piece.   A. E. L.
SEE ALSO: CRYSTAL, EXPANSION

Ice ages see Glacial ages, Geologic time table

✳ **THINGS TO DO**

WHAT EFFECT DOES SALT HAVE ON THE FREEZING POINT OF ICE?

1 Put a tin can inside of a metal pail. Put a layer of chipped ice on the bottom of the pail. Rest the smaller can filled with milk on this layer. Keep adding chipped ice around the inside can until it is level with the top. Put a circle of aluminum foil over the whole surface.

2 Occasionally observe the condition of the inside can. How long does it take the milk to start to freeze?

3 Repeat the experiment a second time. This time add several tablespoons of rock or table salt on every inch layer of ice chips.

4 How long does it take the milk to freeze now? Why? For a solid (salt crystals) to be changed to a solution, heat is necessary. Where does the heat come from?

This large iceberg was sighted from the decks of the Glomar Challenger research vessel.

(vertical caption) Tom Wiley: Scripps Institution of Oceanography

Iceberg Icebergs are giant blocks of ice floating in the sea. They break from continental GLACIERS where the ice reaches the sea. The breaking away of this glacier ice to form icebergs is termed *calving*.

Almost all of the icebergs found in the Northern Hemisphere are from the glacial ice of Greenland. As the ice calves, it is carried by ocean currents into the North Atlantic Ocean in the area of Labrador and Newfoundland. During the summer, when the largest number of icebergs are present, they are a serious danger to shipping.

Icebergs in the Northern Hemisphere may be more than 1 mile (1.6 kilometers) long and hundreds of feet or meters high. Even at this height, only about one eighth of the iceberg shows above the waterline. This makes them difficult to detect.

Today many nations working together in an International Ice Patrol warn shippers of icebergs.   H.S.G.
SEE ALSO: INTERNATIONAL GEOPHYSICAL YEAR, GLACIERS

Igneous rock see Rocks

Ignition see Automobile, Engine

Iguana see Lizard

Ileum see Digestive system

Ilium see Skeleton

Illumination see Bulb, electric; Light

Image see Eye; Lens, man-made

Immunity Immunity is the condition of being able to resist a particular disease. It may be developed *artificially*.

One way is by introducing a different but related disease into the body (like immunity to SMALLPOX from an injection of cowpox virus). Another is to give greatly weakened but live disease GERMS by mouth (like the polio VACCINE) or by injection (like measles, mumps, and German measles). Both methods depend on ANTIBODIES forming in the bloodstream, giving permanent immunity. A third method, for rapid protection, is to give the SERUM of an animal immune to the disease (as in tetanus horse serum). However, people can have allergic reactions to animal serum. If everyone were immunized, many so-called "childhood diseases" might never be problems. H.K.S./E.S.S.
SEE ALSO: GAMMA GLOBULIN

Impala see Antelope

Impatiens see Touch-me-not

Impetigo (imm-puh-TYE-goh) Impetigo is an acute contagious INFECTION of the SKIN. It is caused by either streptococcus or staphylococcus BACTERIA.

It commonly starts on the face as soft blisters which break and drain a clear fluid. This dries to form a yellowish crust on a red background. The sores itch and can be spread by scratching. Contaminated washcloths or towels can pass the infection to others. ANTIBIOTICS in the form of salves and injections are useful in treatment.
SEE ALSO: INFECTION, SKIN

Impetus see Inertia, Motion

Imprinting Imprinting is a form of learning during a very short period in the early life of an animal.

Imprinting sets the permanent behavior pattern of an animal when it relates to a different animal or to an object. Imprinting can occur in chicks *only* during the first three days after hatching. A monkey isolated from others at birth does not have normal adult relations with its own species later.   H.J.C.
SEE ALSO: ANIMAL BEHAVIOR; LORENZ, KONRAD

✳ **THINGS TO DO**

MAKING AN INCUBATOR FOR CHICKEN EGGS

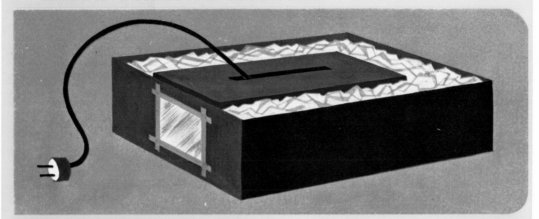

1   Take two cardboard boxes, one large and one small. Cut a small square window in a side of the large box. Then cut a slit on top the small box and suspend an electric bulb with a long cord in the box.

2   Put the small box inside the larger one and pack crumpled newspaper between them on all sides for insulation. Be sure that the open end of the small box fits against the side of the large box in which the window was cut. Place a thermometer in the box so that you can read it through the window. Fit a glass plate over the window. Place a small dish of water in the incubator for moisture.

3   It is necessary to keep the temperature at 103°F (40°C) both night and day for 21 days. Experiment using different bulbs and changing the amount of newspaper, until the incubator has remained at this temperature for a full day.

4   Then put a dozen fertile hen's eggs in the incubator. Turn the eggs daily. After the baby chicks hatch out transfer them to a homemade brooder. They can be supplied with mash and fresh water daily.   **P.G.B.**

Impulse   In biology, an impulse is a stimulus carried through a nerve or a muscle. The stimulus either causes or limits an activity in the body.

In physics, an impulse is either a surge of electrical current, or a change in MOMENTUM which is measured by multiplying the average of the force by the time during which it acts.
SEE: NERVE CELL, NERVOUS SYSTEM, REFLEX

Inbreeding see Hybridization

Incandescent lamp see Bulb, electric

Incendiary bomb see Bombs

Inchworm see Worms

Incisor see Teeth

Inclined plane see Machines, simple

Incubator   A poultry incubator is a large box with glass windows at the front and with trays inside to hold the eggs until they hatch. The incubator takes the place of the mother hen who sits on the eggs to keep them warm. When the chicks hatch and break out of the eggs, they go toward the light at the front of the incubator and are removed.

The first two days eggs are placed in an incubator, the heat is kept at 102° F. (39° C.), and then raised to 103° F. (40° C.). From the third day until two days before the eggs hatch, the eggs are turned twice each day to make sure they are heated the same all over. Incubators hatch thousands of eggs at once in large hatcheries.

Human babies who are born before they

are full size are put into incubators until they gain enough weight to keep their body temperatures at the proper level. Baby incubators are glass boxes. One end can be opened to feed and care for the premature baby. Oxygen is controlled so that the infant receives the proper amount.   P.G.B.

Index fossil see Fossils, Paleontology

Indian paintbrush see Wild flowers

Indian summer Indian summer is a name given to a period of perhaps a week of warm weather in middle or late autumn, usually after the first frost. It results when a polar air mass is converted into a stationary high pressure area.

SEE: AIR MASS, HIGH PRESSURE CENTER

Indigestion Indigestion is not a disease in itself but a group of symptoms such as heartburn, belching or an overfull feeling resulting from impairment of digestion. It may be a nervous affliction or a disease symptom.

Indigo see Dye

Indium Indium is a soft, silvery, metal element. It is as rare as silver and occurs in minerals with zinc, iron, and lead ores. It gets its name from *indigo blue,* the color of some of its salts.

Indium (symbol In) is element number 49. It has an atomic weight of 114.82. It was discovered in 1863 in the ore zincblende by F. Reich and H. Richter.

The United States, Canada, Germany and Belgium are the leading producers of this metal. It is used as a coating to help BEARINGS resist acids and abrasions. It is present in some metal ALLOYS. Compounds of indium are used in transistors and in solar batteries.   V. B. I.

SEE ALSO: ELEMENTS, TRANSISTOR

Inductance coil An inductance coil consists of a number of turns of wire wound on an iron core or nonmetallic tube. The coil is a major part used in electronic circuits to oppose the passage of alternating or varying current. It has no effect on direct current. Coil inductance is measured in *henrys.* A coil has an inductance of one henry when a current change of one ampere per second produces a counter electromotive force of one volt in the coil.

As current starts to flow through a coil and builds up in intensity, an expanding magnetic field is produced. The changing field crosses the wires of the coil and induces an ELECTROMOTIVE FORCE (sort of an electron "push") opposing the current flow. After the current has overcome the opposing force, it starts to decrease in value; but the reversed action of the collapsing magnetic field induces an electromotive force to slow the current. When the current is steady, no expanding or collapsing field is produced and, therefore, no induced voltage retards the flow of electrical current.

The strength of an inductance coil depends upon the size of the wire, the number of turns, the spacing between turns, and the presence of an iron or air core.   E. I. D.

SEE ALSO: ELECTRICITY, INDUCTION

Induction Induction is the effect of producing an electromotive force in a conductor by a change in the electromagnetic field around the conductor.

Even after electric cells and storage batteries had been invented, it was still necessary to find a method of producing large amounts of ELECTRICITY.

In the early part of the 19th century, a Danish teacher named HANS CHRISTIAN OERSTED tried an experiment. He wound wire around a spool and sent a current of electricity through it. The wire then had a field of force like that of a MAGNET.

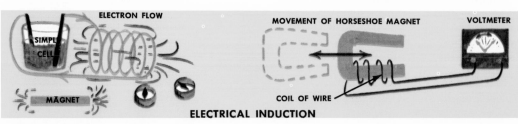

ELECTRON FLOW · SIMPLE CELL · MAGNET · MOVEMENT OF HORSESHOE MAGNET · VOLTMETER · COIL OF WIRE

ELECTRICAL INDUCTION

A few years later, an Englishman named William Sturgeon discovered that if a piece of iron were placed within a coil of wire and an electric current were sent through the wire, the iron became magnetized.

Another Englishman, MICHAEL FARADAY, experimented with a magnet to produce an electric voltage. Using a horseshoe-shaped magnet he thrust one end into a coil of wire and noticed that electricity flowed in one direction in the wire. When the magnet stopped moving, electricity stopped flowing. When he removed the magnet, electricity flowed in the opposite direction.

The fact that an electrical voltage develops whenever a magnetic field changes has become the basis of electrical generators, transformers, and the entire art of radio. V. B. I.
SEE ALSO: DYNAMO

Inelastic collision see Momentum

Inert gas see Elements, Gas

Inertia Inertia is the property of matter which keeps a body at rest unless a force is exerted on it. Inertia also keeps a moving body moving at the same speed and in the same direction unless a force changes the motion.

A person sitting in a parked automobile is pushed back into the seat as the automobile suddenly starts forward. This is due to inertia. As the moving automobile comes to a quick stop, the person continues to move forward, possibly right out of the seat, because no force is applied to stop his forward motion.

SIR ISAAC NEWTON (1642-1727), one of the greatest scientists of all times, was the first to state the three laws of motion. His first law was the *law of inertia*. Inertia obeys the mathematical formula stated by Newton in his second law:

$$F = m \times a$$

In the formula, *F* is the force, such as a push or a pull. Force has the ability to change the motion (in direction or speed), or to set a mass in motion. The *m* is the MASS or amount of matter in a body. The mass of a body is usually determined by measuring its weight at a definite place on the earth's surface. Although mass and weight are both measured in pounds, the weight of a body will lessen as the body is raised in altitude, while the mass will re-

A quick yank on the cart will pull it from under the blocks. The inertia of the blocks prevents them from moving along with it

main the same at any altitude. Weight varies with gravitational force, but mass does not. The letter *a* represents ACCELERATION or the rate of change in velocity. Acceleration can be measured in feet per second.

In the metric system acceleration is usually measured in seconds squared, cm/sec^2 or m/sec^2. For example, a 10-kilogram ball is accelerated at 10 meters per second squared, the force of the ball is 100 newtons. A.J.H.
SEE ALSO: FORCES, GRAVITY, MOTION.

Infantile paralysis see Poliomyelitis

Infection The body is covered by SKIN on the outside. It is covered by MUCOUS MEMBRANE on the inside, from the mouth through the intestines. These protective covers prevent germs from entering the body tissues. If a scratch or a tear occurs in these covers, germs can enter the body. When this happens, infection may develop. Infection may be caused by a VIRUS, BACTERIA, or PARASITE.

When bacteria gain entrance to the tissues beneath the skin, they start to multiply and produce swelling, redness, and soreness of the tissues. The body reacts by sending in millions of white blood corpuscles which surround and destroy the clumps of bacteria. If the white cells are successful in containing the bacteria, the infection remains localized and

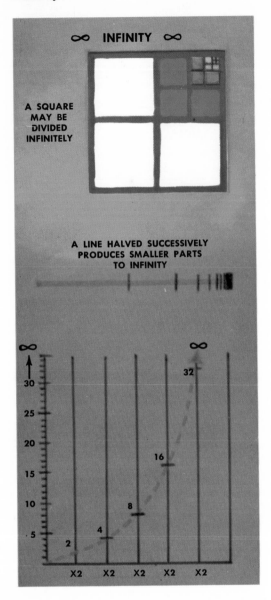

∞ INFINITY ∞

A SQUARE
MAY BE
DIVIDED
INFINITELY

A LINE HALVED SUCCESSIVELY
PRODUCES SMALLER PARTS
TO INFINITY

X2   X2   X2   X2   X2

Infinity Infinity is an unlimited, boundless, unmeasurable extent of time, space, or quantity.

In MATHEMATICS, the positive integers 1, 2, 3, and so on are an example of a *quantity* which has no end. Integers are formed by beginning with number one, adding one to that number for the next number, one to that for the next number, etc. There is no limit to this process because mathematical rules say any two numbers can be added. Therefore, the number of integers, if written in order 1, 2, 3, is infinite or endless.

When a number is divided by a series of numbers which grows smaller and smaller, the quotient grows endlessly larger as the divisor grows endlessly smaller. In the case of a function defined by $y = \dfrac{1}{x}$, as x approaches 0, y approaches infinity. ∞ is the mathematical symbol for infinity.   E. R. B.

Inflammation Whenever the skin is broken and inside cells are injured, or when germs invade the body, a red feverish swelling or *inflammation* starts. Soreness may come with this change, but it means that the body is attempting to heal the damage.

Recovery promptly starts with a histamine-like substance and other chemicals (proteins and enzymes) being released from certain broken cells, causing the local capillaries to dilate and ooze extra blood and liquid to the injured spot (causing the *redness* and *swelling* seen with inflammation). The gathered blood raises the temperature of the area (*heat* and *pain* are the two other signs of inflammation) and speeds up cell metabolism, so new cells can be formed rapidly and dead cells carried away by the white blood cells (leukocytes) that have also come to the area to engulf and destroy conquered bacteria. The PUS that is seen is composed of dead white cells and millions of bacteria. When the body wins the "war" against the invading germs, extra fluids are drained away by the blood and the plasma-carrying lymphatic vessels. Then healing can be completed.

An important step in healing is the IMMUNITY reaction of the body cells. They produce and pour forth special chemicals,

is called an *abcess* or *boil*. If the bacteria overpower the white corpuscles and ANTIBODIES, the infection will spread throughout the tissue and may enter the bloodstream. Then *blood poisoning* may develop.

Bacteria or viruses inhaled into an injured LUNG may produce PNEUMONIA. Certain bacteria can invade the intestine and produce DYSENTERY, such as in TYPHOID FEVER. A mosquito may put parasites in the bloodstream and cause MALARIA. Worms may cause a disease such as TRICHINELLOSIS, which comes from eating pork not cooked thoroughly.   B. M. H.

SEE ALSO: ANTIBIOTICS, BLOOD, INFLAMMATION, MEDICINE, PARASITE, SULFA DRUGS

or *antibodies,* that destroy many germs, thus saving many white cells from the need to engulf *(phagocytize)* them.

Not all inflammations involve bacteria. The normal healing after a germ-free operation, called *sterile healing,* still includes most of the steps just described. Surgically cut and killed cells still need to be removed and repair tissue needs to grow.

Inflammations may carry medical names ending in *-itis.* Examples are appendicitis, tonsilitis, arthritis, and neuritis.   D.A.B./E.S.S.
SEE ALSO: GRANULATION

Influenza Influenza is a disease of the air passages. It usually attacks large numbers of people at about the same time, coming in more severe waves every four or five years. The individual victim is attacked in a few hours with an INFLAMMATION of the membranes of the nose, throat, and breathing tubes.

The onset of "flu" is accompanied by a moderate FEVER. There is a discharge from the nose and throat, and a feeling of weakness with aching in the muscles of the back and legs. Every EPIDEMIC produces a few cases with nausea, vomiting, and a disturbance of the bowels.

Formerly, influenza was called "the grippe." It is known to be caused by a virus that can be identified and cultivated outside the body by incubating it in a hen's egg. There are different strains of "flu" viruses (Hong Kong, Asian, and swine are examples), and they can cause infections of varying severity. Although "flu" by itself is rarely fatal, it can predispose the young, the old, and the weak to fatal pneumonia, and thus causes the death rate to rise.

Since there is no known cure, emphasis has been on the development of vaccines to give yearly to an "at risk" population, but it is often hard to predict which strain will cause an epidemic in any given year. Better, longer-acting vaccines are needed.
H.K.S./E.S.S.
SEE ALSO: INFECTION, VIRUS

Infrared Astronomical Satellite (IRAS) This satellite's mission is to produce an infrared sky map and to catalog up to 1,000,000 infrared sources. By March 1981 it will be in a 559-mile (900-kilometer) polar orbit.

The IRAS is an international satellite, involving a telescope made in the United States, a spacecraft of the Explorer class from the Netherlands, and control facilities operated at Chilbolton, England. The National Aeronautics and Space Administration's (NASA) Caltech Jet Propulsion Laboratory in Pasadena, California, is managing the project.

The primary instrument of the 1,838-pound (834-kilogram) spacecraft is a 24-inch (60-centimeter) Cassegrain telescope. It will be launched from Lompoc, California, with a Delta rocket. Nearly 500 scientists, engineers, and technicians will be involved in the year-long mapping program of infrared regions of the sky that are unobservable from the Earth's surface.

Two astronomical research areas will be studied. In *galactic astronomy,* the infrared search will focus on the origin, constitution, and replenishment of interstellar MATTER, both gas and grains; the problem of STAR formation; and the energy balance in ionized hydrogen regions and molecular clouds. In *extragalactic research,* the infrared search will allow studies of stars being born, aging, and dying. Scientists will also hunt for an infrared radiation shell believed to be expanding since the beginning of time when the "Big Bang" primeval event occured 10 billion years ago.   D.D.
SEE ALSO: ASTRONOMY, SATELLITE, UNIVERSE

Infrared ray see Electromagnetic spectrum; Ray, infrared

Inheritance of characteristics see Heredity

Injection see Drugs, Hypodermic

Ink Ink is a colored liquid or paste-like substance used for writing, printing or drawing on various surfaces. All inks have two things in common. They all have a *liquid* substance for ease of use and they all have *coloring* matter. Ink was first used in China and India as far back as 2500 B. C. Egyptian scholars developed the use of ink further in more recent times.

✳ **THINGS TO DO**

TRY WRITING A LETTER WITH HOMEMADE INK

1 **Two materials are necessary to make ink, iron sulfate and tannic acid. If commercial materials are not available, an iron compound can be made by first soaking some iron nails in carbon tetrachloride to remove the grease coating on them. Put the nails in white vinegar and let them stand for two days. You now have a solution of iron acetate. To make a concentrated solution of tannic acid, boil three tablespoons of tea leaves in a half cup of water.**

2 **Combine equal amounts of the iron acetate and tannic acid. This is ink. It is too thin to write with so mix a small amount of glue into it to make the solution thicker.**

3 **What color is the solution? Write a letter. Let it stand for a day. Now what color is the ink? Commercial ink has soluble dyes added to it so you can see what you write.**

Writing and drawing inks have many different formulas and uses. Inks will vary depending on the degree of permanence desired. Various chemicals and strong dyes are combined to give greater permanence.

The ballpoint pen has recently achieved widespread use. New inks, similar to printing inks, have been developed so that the ink will flow over the ball properly as it is applied to the paper.

Printing inks must serve many different types of printing, such as letterpress, gravure, offset lithography, and electrostatic processes. Each process requires different inks with widely varying properties.

Newspaper black ink is the most widely used. In other forms of commercial printing much color is used and varying problems of paper absorption and drying characteristics must be considered. Other chemicals, in addition to the basic liquid and pigments, are added to meet these special problems.

In all forms of printing the process is mainly one of spreading the ink widely and evenly over a series of rollers for a thin, even application to the printing surface. Quite often ovens or drying agents are used to help in setting and drying ink.

Electrostatic and fluorescent inks are among more recent developments. Electrostatic properties are imparted to both ink and paper to cause the pigment to adhere to the printing surface. Fluorescent materials may be added to some for brilliance and greater visibility at night.   D. A. B.
SEE ALSO: PRINTING

Inoculation see Immunity, Vaccine

Inorganic Inorganic describes materials such as rocks and minerals without living parts and functions. Plants and animals are organic in every cycle, even in decay when their substance returns to the soil and undergoes bacterial changes.

Insecta An insect is any one of more than 850,000 kinds of small, six-legged animals in class Insecta. Insects have a hard skeleton on the outside of their bodies. Some insect adults are wingless but most kinds have four stiff wings. A few kinds, including the flies, bear only two wings.

There are so many kinds of insects that scientists have arranged them in 20 to 25 great groups or orders. Some kinds live in each of almost every kind of place on earth; but few can live in the oceans.

Insects have three body sections: a head, a thorax, and an abdomen. The head bears two *feelers* (antennae), two *compound eyes,* and either side-acting jaws or else piercing and sucking mouthparts. The thorax (chest

The firebrat (left), which resembles the silverfish, is a primitive insect. It does not undergo a metamorphosis from the larval stage. Instead, the young is a miniature of the adult. The milkweed bugs (right) are between the advanced insects, such as the "June bug," and the primitive insects. It goes through an incomplete metamorphosis, in which there is no larval stage. Instead, there is a nymph which resembles a small adult without wings.

A caterpillar is not a worm. It is an immature insect. It is the larval stage in the metamorphosis that creates a butterfly, of order *Lepidoptera*

A cockroach, a member of the order *Orthoptera*, is a household pest. It has been suspected of being a germ carrier

Buchsbaum photos

Army ants, of order *Hymenoptera*, are considered pests. They travel in such great numbers that they cause widespread destruction

The Japanese beetle, belonging to order *Coleoptera*, is a scarab beetle. The adult and larvae have caused great damage to plants

HOW MANY DIFFERENT VARIETIES OF INSECTS CAN YOU IDENTIFY?

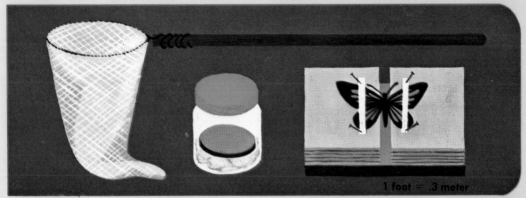

1 foot = .3 meter

An insect collector needs several field tools to aid him in procuring an extensive display of these animals.

1 In order to capture insects a net must be constructed. Sew a two-foot long sack of netting to a circle of wire fashioned from a hanger. Bind the ends of the hanger around an old broom handle and tack the wire in place. The insects caught in the net must then be transferred to a killing jar.

2 A broad-mouthed peanut butter jar makes a good container for this purpose. Put a layer of cotton soaked in carbon tetrachloride in the bottom and cover the cotton with a cardboard disk. This keeps the insects from getting soaked. Leave the insects in the killing jar overnight.

3 Butterflies and moths should be pinned on a spreading board in order to dry their wings in a spread formation. A spreading board can be made by nailing two stacks of several layers of heavy cardboard to a wooden base, leaving a small groove down the center. The body of the insect lies in the groove and the wings are spread over the cardboard and pinned down with little strips of paper.

4 All other insects may be mounted on pins or placed directly on a cotton layer in a flat box. Cover the box with glass or clear plastic. A few moth balls should be put under the cotton to prevent other insects from destroying your collection.

region) bears the six jointed legs and the wings. The abdomen holds the main internal organs, including the digestive tube, kidney-like organs, reproductive organs, and a kind of bagpipe-like, open-ended heart.

Insects have a well-developed nervous system and a tiny brainlike *ganglion* located inside the head above the mouth. Two main nerves extend around and beneath the mouth to join into a second brain mass; and from there, nerve cords go down the *underside* of the thorax and abdomen.

Insects' nerves and sense organs work well, as we note when a fly escapes our moving hands. Bees and roaches can learn limited new habits; and bees can detect ultraviolet "colors" of flowers to which human eyes are blind. But most insect behavior is unchangeable or *instinctual:* a wasp always builds a certain shape of nest.

Life cycles: Insects develop in one of two ways. In one type of life cycle, the egg hatches as a worm-like *larva* (in certain species called a grub, maggot, caterpillar, or "worm"). After the larva eats, grows, and sheds its skin several times, it changes to a resting *pupa* (or cocoon) stage. Later, the pupal case splits and out comes an adult. This is *complete metamorphosis*.

In *incomplete* metamorphosis, the egg hatches as a small, adult-like stage, a *nymph* —a tiny wingless copy of its parents; and it slowly grows and sheds to become a full-winged adult, as a grasshopper or bug.

Millions of dollars of damage occur each year from such destroyers as cotton weevils, corn borers, clothes moths, fruit-tree pests, and disease-bearing flies. But great values come to man from honey bees, flower-pollinating insects, and the many kinds that are food for wildlife. D. A. B.

SEE ALSO: ARTHROPODA, MOLTING

Insecticides Insecticides are poisonous chemicals used to kill insects. Their use protects men's food supply and forests from harmful insects and prevents the spread of insect-borne diseases.

To use insecticides correctly, one needs a full understanding of the feeding habits and the life histories of the insect pests.

Stomach poisons are used against leaf-chewing insects such as grasshoppers and the caterpillars of destructive moths. The leaves of the insect's food plants are sprayed with the poison. Examples of common stomach insecticides are *paris green* and *lead arsenate*.

Contact poisons are used to kill sucking insects such as APHIDS, and true BUGS. Stomach poisons are not effective on them since they suck plant juices by piercing the plant surfaces down to the xylem and phloem tissues beneath. Examples of contact poisons are oil emulsions with NICOTINE and lime-sulfur solution. The newest insecticides of this type are the *systemic* insecticides which are sprayed on the plants and which then enter the xylem-phloem circulation and make every part of the plant poisonous. Still these new chemicals do not harm the plants themselves.

Fumigants are readily evaporated liquids or gases like carbon disulfide or the deadly hydrocyanic acid. They kill by entering the insects' breathing tubes (tracheae.) Peach borer larvae, the pink bollworm, and common clothes moths can be controlled by fumigants. Unfortunately, they require expert handling and are effective only in enclosed spaces.

Spray insecticides act by clogging or poisoning through the tracheae of insects. Pyrethrum powder and certain chemically-treated oils are sprayed onto plants in still air. Sprays are used to control such insects as cabbage worm, tussock moth larva, and cotton boll weevil.

Recently, scientists have isolated a hormone secreted by a gland near an insect's brain. Normally this gland stops functioning as an insect develops into an adult. Using an insecticide made of this juvenile hormone will keep insects from "growing up." The nymph of a milkweed bug will just become

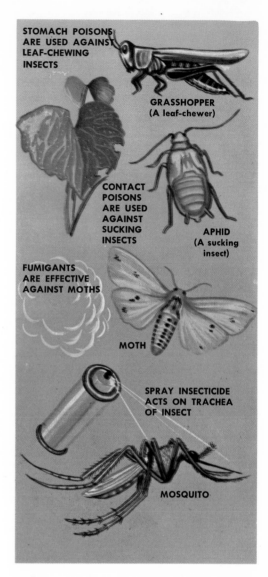

STOMACH POISONS ARE USED AGAINST LEAF-CHEWING INSECTS

GRASSHOPPER (A leaf-chewer)

CONTACT POISONS ARE USED AGAINST SUCKING INSECTS

APHID (A sucking insect)

FUMIGANTS ARE EFFECTIVE AGAINST MOTHS

MOTH

SPRAY INSECTICIDE ACTS ON TRACHEA OF INSECT

MOSQUITO

a giant nymph. A mealworm pupa will develop into a short-lived second pupa instead of an adult. This technique will prevent insect larvae from maturing into harmful adults.

Man is constantly faced with the problem of insects being transported from one country to another by aircraft. The World Health Organization Assembly is requesting that all international jets use an odorless dichlorous spray while in flight. A thirty minute application kills insects but will not harm humans. This insecticide will be used in flights that go and come from tropical regions.

The current controversy over the harmful effects of insecticides on wildlife and humans is causing man to turn to other methods of insect control. One method is sterilization. This would eliminate the destruction of useful insects.

HEDGEHOG

SHORT-TAILED SHREW

MOLE

Insectivore (in-SECK-tuh-vore)
Insectivore is the name of a group of
animals that live primarily on insects.
These little furry animals usually live
underground and come out at night to
search for insects. Their sharp claws
are used for digging tunnels in the soil.
Shrews, moles, and hedgehogs belong
to this group.

Insectivores have sharp teeth, which they
use to break the hard outer shells of insects.
Most have scent glands. Their strong odor
keeps bigger animals away from them.

Insectivores are found in the temperate
and tropical climates. Some live on water
insects instead of burrowing underground
for insects. The otter shrew lives in the
rivers of tropical Africa. The golden mole
also lives in Africa. Its forefeet are very
large and scooplike. Golden moles are dark
brown or gray with a purple sheen.

The *shrew* is the smallest mammal alive.
It spends most of its life fighting and eating,
often eating eight times its weight in 24
hours. Its poison glands are useful in getting
food but the dose is too tiny to hurt man.
The female gives birth to 15 to 20 offspring
in three litters a year.

The *hedgehog* ranges in size from 6 to 8
inches (15.2 to 20.3 centimeters). If it is
annoyed, it will roll into a ball and project its
quills. It can swim a short distance if forced
to do so. Its elongated snout is a handy tool
to dig out insects, preferably ants.

The following mammals eat insects and
may be called insectivorous, but they are
not in the order Insectivora. Small bats
catch insects on the wing at dusk or night.
They will discard parts of insects not tasty.
Pangolins and aardwolves feast on termites.
Anteaters relish ants and will eat a pound
(.5 kilogram) at one meal.   H.J.C.

Insectivorous plants see Plants, insectivorous

Insight Insight is a form of learning
that occurs when an animal reasons
out a solution to a new problem or
situation. No trial and error period is
involved.

A chimpanzee is put in a room with
bananas hanging out of his reach. He will
take the boxes scattered around the room,
stack them up, and climb to get the food.
This is an example of insight. Some
classifiers also place the use of language in
this type of ANIMAL BEHAVIOR.   H.J.C.

Insoluble (inn-SAUL-yuh-buhl) Insoluble is a term referring to a substance which is difficult to dissolve. It
is difficult to get the molecules to dis-
perse in a medium to form a homogeneous mixture. No substance is
completely insoluble.
SEE: DISPERSION, SOLUTION

Inspiration Inspiration, or inhaling,
is the process of drawing air into the
LUNGS. It is the opposite of *expiration*.
SEE: RESPIRATORY SYSTEM

Instinct Instinct is an *inborn* response,
a force which causes an organism to
react and adapt its behavior to its environment in a way characteristic of
its species. Instinct is thought to be
both inherited and dependent on the
growth of the organism's systems. It
has not been adequately explained by
science. An example of an instinct is
the automatic searching for food of a
new-born animal.
SEE: PSYCHOLOGY

**Certain pigeons have the instinct always to
return to their home cages.**

Instrument landing system dial

Rockwell International

The various dials on the instrument panel give pilots readings on altitude and speed.

Instrument landing system

The instrument landing system is a set of instruments, radio stations, and receivers which help AIRPLANE pilots guide their planes to safe landings in bad weather. The instrument landing system, or ILS, makes a pathway of radio signals for the pilot.

In the cockpit, a pilot has two small lights and an ILS instrument dial. These are operated by receivers in the aircraft which pick up signals from transmitters on the ground.

One of the ground transmitters sends out a flat beam of radio energy, straight out from the runway, and at an upward angle. This beam is called the *glide path.* Another station sends a vertical wall of radio waves called the *localizer beam.*

The pilot's ILS dial has two needles, one vertical, the other horizontal. When the needles are crossed in the center of the dial, the pilot knows that he is flying down the glide path and straight through the localizer beam. The needles move to show him when he is off course.

A small transmitter at the end of the runway and another one 5 miles (8 kilometers) from the end of the runway send beams straight up. When the pilot flies through the beam of the beacon five miles from the airport, one of the lights in the cockpit flashes. When he gets to the airport, the other transmitter flashes the second light. These transmitters are called the *outer marker* and the *inner marker,* respectively.

ILS is used by both military and civilian airports and aircraft. Most major airports have ILS equipment, and most airliners and many small planes have the instruments necessary to use it.   R. J. J.

SEE ALSO: AIRCRAFT; BEAM, RADIO

Instrument panel

By observing the aircraft instrument panel, the airplane pilot knows how the airplane is flying. The instrument panel is like the dashboard of a car. It contains instruments that tell the pilot about speed, altitude, attitude, and course. There also are instruments that tell about the engines. They indicate how fast each engine is running and whether or not everything is working properly. Other instruments show how other parts of the airplane are working.

The instrument panel is in front of the pilot, just as the dashboard of a car is in front of the driver. Small airplanes have small instrument panels with only a few dials. Larger airplanes may have two instrument panels. One is for the pilot, and the other is for the copilot. On very large airplanes there are many instruments.

FLIGHT INSTRUMENTS

Aircraft instrument panels have three groups of instruments. The first are *flight instruments.* From these the pilot can tell how the airplane is moving through the air. For example, the *Turn and Slip Indicator* shows the pilot how fast the airplane is turning, how steeply it is tilted or banked, and whether it is slipping or skidding. The *altimeter* shows how high the airplane is flying. The *Air Speed Indicator* shows how fast the airplane is moving through the air. The *Rate of Climb Indicator* shows how fast the airplane is climbing or descending.

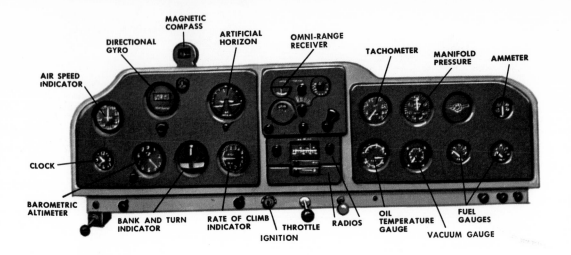

MAGNETIC COMPASS · DIRECTIONAL GYRO · ARTIFICIAL HORIZON · OMNI-RANGE RECEIVER · TACHOMETER · MANIFOLD PRESSURE · AMMETER · AIR SPEED INDICATOR · CLOCK · BAROMETRIC ALTIMETER · BANK AND TURN INDICATOR · RATE OF CLIMB INDICATOR · THROTTLE · IGNITION · RADIOS · OIL TEMPERATURE GAUGE · FUEL GAUGES · VACUUM GAUGE

NAVIGATION INSTRUMENTS

The second group is called the *navigation* group. These instruments tell the pilot about the airplane's path over the ground. A COMPASS is one navigation instrument. The pilot also uses a clock. A *directional gyro* uses a GYROSCOPE to tell the pilot when the airplane is off course. The *VOR receiver* is an instrument connected to a radio receiver. This instrument picks up signals from special Omni-Range radio stations and gives the pilot a course to fly to the destination.

The DME (Distance Measuring Equipment) tells him how far he is from a station.

ENGINE AND SYSTEMS INSTRUMENTS

The instrument panel's third group is the *engine and auxiliary systems* group. Instruments like the Tachometer, Manifold Pressure Gauge, Oil Pressure and Oil Temperature Gauges help the pilot to determine how the engine is behaving. The *Tachometer* indicates the speed of the engine in revolutions per minute or RPM. The *Manifold Pressure Gauge* shows the pressure in the engine's intake manifold. This is a good indication of how much power the engine is developing. *Oil Pressure* and *Oil Temperature* gauges are safety instruments. If anything should go wrong with the engine, these instruments would show that it was not operating normally. If the airplane has jet engines, the instrument panel will have a *Tailpipe Temperature Gauge,* which is a safety instrument. If the temperature of the exhaust becomes too high, there is danger of engine failure or fire.

Auxiliary systems are such things as the landing gear, flaps, lights, pressurization equipment, radios, and hydraulic systems. The instrument panel has indicators that show whether or not these systems are performing their functions properly. These indicators may be round dials like the engine and flight instruments, or they may be warning lights or lights which indicate that all is normal. Some instruments give a sound warning such as a horn blowing if something is wrong. The horn will go off in the cockpit if the pilot tries to land the airplane without lowering the landing gear.

There are usually many switches on the instrument panel. These control parts of the airplane by means of small electric motors called *servos.* Raising and lowering the landing gear and the flaps is accomplished by moving switches on the instrument panel. Using ignition and starter switches, the pilot can start and shut off the engines.

Sometimes it is necessary for the pilot to fly without being able to see the ground. Then the instruments tell the pilot the altitude and position of the airplane, and how to get to the destination. This is called flying "on instruments." At night and in bad weather the instrument panel is lighted. Red lights are usually used, because they do not interfere with the pilot's night vision.

The instrument panel gives a pilot information needed to fly the airplane safely. It makes it possible to know what is going on, even in parts of the airplane that cannot be seen. It makes night flying and flying in bad weather safe. Its many dials, gauges, lights, and switches appear complicated, but to the experienced pilot, they give a clear picture of how the airplane is performing, where it is, and how to get to the destination. R.J.J.

SEE ALSO: AIRPLANE, INSTRUMENT LANDING SYSTEM

Insulator Any material which will not conduct ELECTRICITY or heat is an insulator. Among the best materials for electrical insulation are AMBER, sulfur, MICA, rubber, GLASS, and some PLASTICS.

Resinous or vitreous (glass-like) substances are generally good insulators and poor conductors (substances that will not allow an electric current or heat to pass through them). Metals such as copper, gold, silver, and steel are poor insulators and good conductors. A. E. L.

SEE ALSO: HEAT, HEAT BARRIERS, RUBBER, SULFUR

Insulin Insulin is a hormone produced by the ISLETS OF LANGERHANS in the pancreas. It is absorbed directly into the blood. Insulin regulates the burning of SUGAR by the body.

These small protein molecules are used in the treatment of DIABETES mellitus. It cannot be swallowed; digestive enzymes destroy it. Researchers are trying to make a tiny artificial pancreas that can be inserted into the body. It would be sensitive to blood sugar level and trip off the release of insulin that would be stored in a small reservoir. Commercial insulin is extracted from pigs, sheep, and cattle. H.J.C.

SEE ALSO: BANTING, EDWARD; ENDOCRINE GLANDS

Intake valve see Engine

Integer see Arithmetic, Infinity, Number systems

Integumentary system The integumentary system is the coating or protective covering of any organism. In zoology, it is the shell or skin of an animal. In botany, the integumentary system is a rind, shell or skin protecting the fruit or seed.

SEE: EPITHELIAL TISSUE

Interdependence see Balance of nature, Ecosystem

Internal combustion engine see Automobile, Engine

Internal medicine Internal medicine is the branch or specialty in medicine that deals with diagnosis and treatment of diseases of the internal organs. Doctors in this field are called *internists.*

Not until the 1880s did doctors who were interested in learning more about the causes of certain diseases take additional training beyond medical school. Today an internist completes at least three years of training after medical school as a *resident physician* at a hospital. The first year of this training was once called an *internship,* and the doctor was called an *intern.* After residency, a doctor might take an extra year of training (called a *fellowship*) in a subspecialty of internal medicine. Some of these are *cardiology,* the study of HEART and blood vessel diseases; *rheumatology,* the study of ARTHRITIS and related disorders of the connective tissue; *gastroenterology,* the diagnosis and treatment of disorders of the ALIMENTARY CANAL; and *nephrology,* the study of KIDNEY diseases.

Internists do not perform surgery. They are considered *diagnosticians.* They talk to a patient (take his or her health history), order appropriate laboratory tests, and perform a physical examination. From the information they assemble, like putting clues together to solve a mystery, they determine what is wrong and how best to treat the patient. Because of this skill, other doctors often refer their medical "problem patients" to an internist.

One out of five new doctors chooses to specialize in internal medicine. It is the foundation of *primary care* of patients. Most people who are ill consult either an internist, a *family physician* (once called a practitioner), or a *pediatrician* (If a child is ill). There must be close cooperation among these primary care specialists so the patient's total health needs are considered. In internal medicine, new ways to treat and diagnose illness are constantly being developed. Those who specialize in each field try to help other doctors keep informed. E.S.S.

SEE ALSO: PATHOLOGY

International Bureau of Weights and Measures The International Bureau of Weights and Measures was formed in

France in 1875. There were 17 nations present at the start. The present bureau has about 44 nations.

The bureau meets at least once every six years at Pavillon de Breteuil, a royal palace at Sevres near Paris, France. The Director of the National Bureau of Standards represents the United States.

The bureau is the governing body for the METRIC SYSTEM. It controls the revision and the extension of the metric system. The bureau establishes the basis for each of the basic units. It also prevents the proliferation of unnecessary units.   A.J.H.

SEE ALSO: INTERNATIONAL SYSTEM OF UNITS, MEASUREMENT, METRIC SYSTEM

International Control of Natural Resources

A nation cannot exist alone. The world is too small, and the environment of one nation is also that of others. Sewage dumped into waters on one shore finds its way to the coastline of another country. Pollution poured into the skies gets blown to other continents. Radioactive materials are carried around the world. Biocides and heavy metals show up in fishes caught by foreign nets in polluted waters. Water, air, and life are precious natural resources, and cooperation among all people to preserve them is imperative.

Many nations agree that conservation and control measures on a number of products, plants, and animals are international problems. These are concerns that cut across political boundaries. Therefore, the conservation of natural resources must be considered on an international scale.

In 1948 the UNESCO program of the United Nations created the International Union for Conservation of Nature and Natural Resources (IUCN) to act as the major conservation organization of the world. The main purpose of the IUCN is to promote or support action that will ensure the protection of wild nature and natural resources on a worldwide scale. The main area of concern deals with the conservation of plants, animals, the soil, water, air, and other resources that constitute the basic wealth of the earth. They also work toward protecting animals that are in danger of extinction, maintaining natural habitats for wild animals, and encouraging the establishment of national parks and wildlife refuge areas.

NATURAL RESOURCES

Because of the rapid growth of science and technology over the past 50 years, the world's supply of natural resources has been seriously depleted. Industrialized nations have exploited known sources of natural resources at an extraordinary rate, and we are steadily running short of many important resources. Many economies depend on petroleum, coal, and iron ore, and the availability of enormous quantities of water. Most natural resources are nonrenewable, and once these reserves have been exhausted, there can be no more.

One of the more pressing problems is the future supply of petroleum and natural gas. The ENERGY CRISIS of 1973 showed clearly that the world is running low on FOSSIL FUELS, and the time to regulate energy uses and develop new sources of energy is now.

ENDANGERED SPECIES

The International Union for the Conservation of Nature and Natural Resources provides a list of endangered species in the world. Called the *Red Book* and updated constantly, this book contains the names of plants and animals that can become extinct if measures aren't taken to preserve them. Most industries buying furs for wearing apparel refuse to purchase skins of animals listed in this book.

Generally people think only animal populations are becoming extinct and give little attention to rare marsh or bog plants that are losing their aquatic *habitat*. Merely listing endangered species does not save them. Direct action to preserve their ECOSYSTEM is needed.

For decades some nations have participated in drawing up agreements or treaties related to endangered species. As early as 1918 the Migratory Bird Treaty Act was established. It must be renegotiated from time to time to clarify who owns wildlife, especially migratory species. Certain species of egrets, birds of paradise, and ostriches have been exploited. Can one country that has a booming feather trade destroy birds for economic reasons? Can some countries be permitted to have no hunting regulations or loose ones?

Canada and the United States have entered into six different agreements related to sealing and fishing. This is an obvious arrangement, for we have a joint interest and concern about our common resources. The first seal treaty in 1911 was an attempt to keep fur seals from becoming extinct. In 1957 the Interim Convention on Conservation of North Pacific Fur Seals was held. Russia, United States, Canada, and Japan participated. Baby seals born on islands in the Bering Sea were being clubbed to death for their fur to make coats. Rules were necessary. Usually only adult males can be killed. As herds become overpopulated, adult females may be killed. Each country in the agreement has a limited number of seals that may be killed.

In the early part of the century, whales in the northern Atlantic and Pacific waters were being exploited. As the whale populations diminished, whalers headed for the Antarctic. Finally nations decided an international problem existed because whales are common property.

In the 1940s, the International Whaling Commission was established. Sixteen nations agreed that rules should be laid down. Each country set a quota on killing whales. These quotas were obviously too high; the whole whale population is diminishing. Japan and the Soviet Union are the only two nations today who continue to exploit these mammals. The United States has stopped whaling and will not permit importation of whale products. Eight great whales are in danger of extinction including blue, sperm, and bowhead whales.

International agreements are voluntary, and it is difficult to monitor violators. A ship coming into territorial waters can be seized and examined for infractions of the rules, but this is not enough. Each nation must monitor its own people and live by the

rules, or everyone loses. When our world resources disappear, so will humans.

P.P.S./H.J.C.

SEE ALSO: BALANCE OF NATURE, CONSERVATION OF NATURE

International Date Line The International Date Line is that imaginary line on the Earth at which the calendar changes from one date to the next. It is located in the Pacific Ocean and follows the 180th meridian except where it would cross islands. Where this happens, it curves around each island.

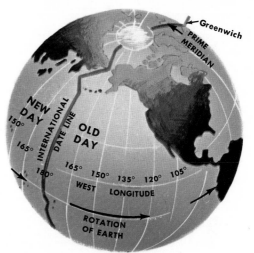

The earth is divided into 24 time zones. To make one complete rotation it turns 360° in 24 hours. This means that each time zone is 15° wide. A traveler going eastward from one time belt to another "loses" an hour with each change of time, while the westward traveler "gains" an hour. At some one place on earth, the beginning of the 24-hour day must be determined. The *International Date Line* was established for this purpose. As a traveler crosses this line, he must make a change of date that makes up for the "losses" or "gains" of time. The traveler moving to the west moves his calendar forward as from July 1 to July 2. The eastward traveler moves his calendar back one day. The International Date Line is located so that it crosses ocean areas only. This means that all changes of time are made on planes or ships at sea and no body of land and no political unit (such as a group of islands) is divided by the Date Line. H. S. G.

SEE ALSO: EARTH, TIME ZONES

For further information write:
World Wildlife Fund, Suite 619, 910 17th St.,
N.W., Washington, D.C. 20006 or United
Nations UNESCO, New York, NY 00017.

International Geophysical Year

Scientists call the study of the physical earth *geophysics,* from the Greek word *ge,* meaning "earth." The earth is always changing. Changes in one part of the earth affect earth as a whole. The eighteen months between July, 1957, to December, 1958, were set aside for scientists to work together and to take observations in order to improve their understanding of the earth and its changes. This period of time was called the *International Geophysical Year—IGY.*

Fotokhronika TASS

A Soviet scientist checks microfilm negatives of weather observations to be sent to the United States.

The major aim of the IGY was to study the rapid and continual changes in earth's atmosphere. Since the atmosphere is greatly influenced by the SUN, the IGY was obliged to study the sun. The influence of oceans and glaciers, and, in particular, the effect of Antarctica on the lower atmosphere, where weather changes occur, were studied. Since groups of scientists worked in areas where the solid earth had been little studied, they were able to make valuable discoveries about the form and composition of the earth's surface and crust.

IGY scientists formed a giant, world-wide organization to plan and coordinate their observations. It was extremely important for simultaneous observation and measurements to be made on carefully standarized instruments so that the complex relationships among the sun, atmosphere, earth, water, and ice could be understood. Four thousand IGY outposts were maintained, including drifting stations, mountain peak observatories, satellites, arctic and antarctic camps. Special world days were selected for more intensive and simultaneous observations. All information was relayed to three *World Data Centers* located in Russia, Western Europe, and the United States. Some of these findings will be discussed in the following articles under the topics *Antarctica, Atmosphere, Glaciers,* and *Solid Earth.*   E.R.B./H.W.M.

International Geophysical Year: Antarctica The IGY work at ANTARCTICA was an example of complete international cooperation.

Twelve nations worked together to set up thirty-five camps from which to explore the earth's little known continent.

Stations observed the aurora, and studied the weather and how it changed; the rays coming from the upper atmosphere; and the depth and structure of ice. The earth under the ice was studied by soundings and magnetic measurements. Many over-ice trips (called *traverses*) were made, some lasting several days, some several weeks. Everywhere the scientists measured, took temperatures, and made observations.

The results showed that there was nearly twice as much ice (40% more) than was thought, but less land under the ice. East Antarctica is indeed a CONTINENT, thickly crusted with mineral rocks over five hundred million years old. West Antarctica is an arc of islands bridged over by ice and separated from East Antarctica by a deep trough. The total land area is about twice the size of the United States. The ice is very thick, averaging 8,000 feet (2,400 meters). There are a few ice-free spots, such as the McMurdo Sound and Cape Hallett, where lichen and moss grow and where glacial deposits have shown that at least three ice ages have occurred in the last one hundred million years. The oldest ice deposits were 2,000 feet (600 meters) above the valley

National Academy of Sciences—IGY photo; Fotokhronika TASS; British Information Service photo

(Left) A British team led by Dr. Vivian Fuchs feels its way to shore through ice floes in Antarctica to rescue 11 marooned British scientists. **(Center)** A portable drill is used by a Russian team in seismic and temperature studies. **(Right)** A seismic explosion is set to determine the thickness of ice in Antarctica. Shock waves travel down to the bedrock and echo back to the surface where they are recorded.

floor, the intermediate about 1,000 feet (300 meters). IGY scientists could not tell by the most recent MORAINES (deposits of sand and gravel left by the glacier) whether the glacier is retreating (melting) or advancing (growing).

The weather in Artarctica is the world's fiercest. The high central South Pole PLATEAU in the middle of East Antarctica is the coldest place on earth, -125° F (-87.2° C.). It reflects ninety per cent of the sun's rays. The coastal areas are warmer. Therefore the cold, dry, dense air flows down toward the coasts as the warmer, moist air moves upward. The earth's rotation causes a *whorl,* or *vortex,* of westerly winds—more intense during the Antarctic winter than summer. Storms are rare in the high interior of East Antarctica where a pole of circulation exists. Some storms cross Antarctica over the transcontinental trough; others continue east over the South Pacific. The most persistent winds are in East Antarctica, about one-third of the distance from the coast. Storms originating in Antarctica affect the weather in the entire Southern Hemisphere.

IGY aurora observations have shown a daily shift due to the motion of the earth's magnetic field. They also show a seasonal effect.

Antarctica has been set aside as an international preserve for scientific research. A treaty, which has been ratified by nearly all nations, says, "It is in the interests of all mankind that Antarctica shall continue forever to be used exclusively for peaceful purposes and shall not become the scene or object of internal discord." Later co-operative studies in progress involve a floating laboratory weather ship, cosmic ray, and magnetic field studies.

An outgrowth of the IGY has been the formation of IGC, *International Geophysical Cooperation.* Planned observations of all the earth's major phenomena are continuing.

H.W.M.

SEE ALSO: AURORA BOREALIS

International Geophysical Year: Atmosphere The sun was studied during the IGY because of its great influence on the atmosphere. A time was chosen when scientists expected the sun to be very active. During this study the SUN staged its most explosive show in 200 years. It was under constant observation from someplace in the world, and it was photographed in new ways which revealed the changes it was going through, never before recorded by man.

Traces of the earth's atmosphere were found at altitudes much higher than before believed to exist. The *corona* of the sun was also found to be much more extensive than formerly believed. This was discovered by the first RADAR signals to be bounced off the corona.

Scientists learned where the invisible rays

of the sun—X rays, ultraviolet rays, and infrared rays—originate, and the effect of each on earth. Indications were found that the sun's *radiation* is increasing. Satellites continue to measure the sun's radiation.

Scientists found that increased solar flare activity on the sun brought about an increase in the amount of cosmic energy received by the earth's atmosphere. A great amount of information about the nature of cosmic rays was gathered, resulting in better understanding of the effects of these rays.

A small part of the earth's magnetic field was found to be generated by globe-circling electric currents in the upper atmosphere called *electrojets*. Since they influence the earth's magnetic field, knowledge of these currents helps in the preparation of navigational maps.

VAN ALLEN BELT

One of IGY's biggest discoveries was the *Van Allen* belt, made by the satellite Explorer I. The Van Allen belt is a region (named for the man responsible for its discovery) containing many electrons and protons that were given off by the sun and trapped in the earth's magnetic field. First discovered was the belt portion down to 1,400 miles (2,250 kilometers) altitude, then the upper region more than 12,000 miles (19,300 kilometers) above the earth. At first it was thought that there was more than one definite belt. It is now known that a single Van Allen belt circles the globe except at the regions of the magnetic poles.

Scientists discovered the reason for the simultaneous occurrence of solar flares and auroras in the polar skies. Auroras were found to occur when solar flares cause the belt to dip into the earth's atmosphere where moving particles in the belt collide with atmospheric gases.

Scientists believe that the Van Allen belt also causes the mysterious magnetic "storms" that occasionally wrap the earth. These seem to occur as a result of solar flares pushing part of the belt into the ionosphere, the electrified atmosphere region high above earth. It contains layers of ions created by solar radiation that strip electrons from atoms and molecules. These layers are used to reflect radio waves back to earth for long distance radio. The belt disturbance causes the ionosphere to absorb, rather than transmit, signals; and radio and radar communications at the North and South poles are completely disrupted.

SATELLITE PROGRAM

The satellite program was part of the world-wide research in the atmosphere. By the mid-1950's, it had become technically possible for both the U.S.S.R. and the U.S. to build and launch an artificial satellite into space. IGY provided the incentive which made possible the money and skill for such a project.

Russia first launched a satellite on Oct. 4, 1957. Two more Russian satellites were put into orbit before the end of IGY. The first IGY-U.S. satellite was launched from Cape Canaveral, Florida, on January 31, 1958. It was designed to measure cosmic ray intensity, density of meteoric matter, and temperatures inside and outside the satellite. The U.S. orbited six more satellites before IGY was over. Volunteers were enlisted to track them, using radio stations, and to transmit any scientific data from satellite instruments to IGY centers.

Rockets were also used as research tools. Rockets studied the sun without its being screened by the atmosphere, and gathered facts about the high atmosphere itself. They were launched at latitudes all the way from the Arctic to the Antarctic.   E.R.B.

SEE ALSO: ATMOSPHERE; AURORA BOREALIS; ELECTRON; IONIZATION; SATELLITE, MANMADE

International Geophysical Year: Glaciers
The ice-covered sections of the earth were also studied during IGY. These sections, located mainly at the North and South pole regions, occupy one-tenth of the area of the globe, and affect world CLIMATE and weather. Whether they are increasing or decreasing is a matter of great importance. In some past ages, the world has been free of ice; in other ages, ice has covered one-third of the globe. During IGY scientists measured glacial changes all over the world, as well as at the poles.

Glaciers are made of snow, gradually packed into ice by the pressure of more snow. Under great pressure, the ice becomes slightly fluid so that glaciers flow

(Top left) This unusual aurora display of a rayed form with an arc was seen in Alaska.

National Academy of Sciences — IGY photo

(Top right) Sunspots, such as this solar protuberance, were studied by IGY.

High Altitude Observatory

(Center) NIKE-ASP high altitude rockets were used to measure radiation during solar flares.

U.S. Navy photo

(Bottom right) Three photos by a satellite tracking camera allowed accurate orbital calculations.

Smithsonian Astrophysical Observatory

slowly down from mountain heights, where they are formed, to lower levels. If they reach the sea, they break off into ICEBERGS, raising the water level. This seems to be happening at the present time. On the other hand, some glaciers (in the northwestern United States) seem to be growing. Continued measurements are needed to determine the true pattern.

Glaciers are a storehouse of past climates. Every snowfall is permanently filed away for future reference under later snowfalls. If melting occurs during the summer, a bluish ice layer tells the tale. To unlock past weather records, scientists drilled deep holes into the ice and removed sample "cores." These were analyzed by oxygen ISOTOPE study methods (rain contains more heavy oxygen than snow) to find whether rain or snow fell at the poles. It has been found that far more snow has fallen in the Arctic than in the Antarctic. The evidence is in the thickness of the core layers.

During IGY two drifting stations (Russia and United States), established on icebergs in the Arctic, were found to move in a clockwise direction around the Pole. This indicated that they were dependent on surface currents driven by the prevailing wind. As they drifted, constant soundings and photographs of the ocean floor were taken. It was found to be rocky and rugged. The temperature of the ocean was found to be rising.

H.W.M.

SEE ALSO: ANTARCTICA; GLACIAL AGES; GLACIER; POLES, NORTH AND SOUTH

NASA

International Geophysical Year: The solid Earth During IGY scientists learned new facts about the size and shape of the EARTH and what it is made of. They learned about the forces at work inside the earth.

One of the tools they used in their studies was gravity. GRAVITY is not the same all over the earth because the earth is not a perfect sphere. Measurements of gravity from place to place reveal much about the shape of the earth, the thickness of its crust, and the elevations and distances between land masses on its surface.

Scientists tried to get complete coverage of gravity measurements from all over the world. The first successful surface measurements in the open sea were done during IGY. Instead of using submarines submerged to quiet depths, gravity measurements were taken in moderately calm seas any place on the ocean surfaces of the earth.

The first complete gravity picture showed that earth is a slightly pear-shaped spheroid with a 45-foot (13.7-meter) bulge at the North Pole. For the first time, LATITUDES and LONGITUDES were determined accurately, as well as exactly how far apart the continents are and where certain islands are.

Gravity measurements and recordings of earthquake waves were used in the studies of the earth's crust and mantle. The *crust* (outside layer) was found to be craggier and more creased than once thought. New hypotheses were formed concerning mountain-building. Scientists formerly thought that the earth was cooling and the crust wrinkling, and that the wrinkles grew into mountains. This theory was discarded when, during IGY, the crust was measured and found not to be thickest under mountains, as this theory demanded. Some scientists now believe that the earth is expanding, cracking in weak places and pushing up mountains in others. The *East Pacific Ridge,* an underwater ridge in the Pacific Ocean which is above water level at the Easter and Galápagos islands, has many active volcanoes, and is one of the hottest spots on the earth's surface. This has led scientists to consider that it is welling up with molten rock from the earth's depths and may someday be dry land. This may be how mountains were formed in the past.

The layers of the *mantle* (that portion of the earth directly under the crust) were mapped during IGY. Scientists think it is divided into four layers, each with different properties. The depth of the mantle is close to 1,800 miles (2,900 kilometers). Below the mantle, at the center of earth, is the *core.* There is an *outer liquid core* and an *inner solid* one. Earth's magnetic field is believed to have originated in the outer core. The conclusions about the layers below the crust were drawn from the study of waves from many earthquakes all over the earth. Special long-period seismometers, which are now recording earthquakes around the world, will continue to provide scientists with information about earth's interior. E.R.B.

SEE ALSO: EARTHQUAKE, OCEANOGRAPHY, PLATE TECTONICS, SEISMOGRAPH

International Hydrological Decade The International Hydrological Decade (1965-1974) was a program of international cooperation designed to attract the attention of the scientific

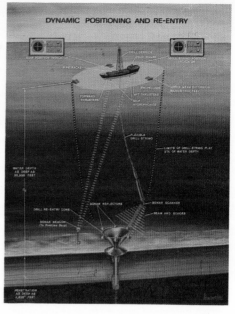

Scripps Institute of Oceanography

(Above) The Glomar Challenger research vessel is helping scientists study the formation of the oceans. It can take samples from the ocean floor through its derrick-enclosed drill atop the ship. (Right) Diagram showing the Glomar Challenger's drilling operation.

community and the population at large to the importance of WATER science. In the United States, research efforts were directed by the Division of Earth Sciences of the National Academy of Sciences. On an international level, 80 countries agreed to participate in research activities under the guidance of UNESCO (United Nations Educational, Scientific, and Cultural Organization).

The Decade program included evaluation of basic data on *hydrology,* inventories, and water balances, along with research and educational projects. Through a series of meetings that were convened at many locations around the world, a wide range of topics was discussed, including regional hydrology of specific areas, physical *limnology,* and artificial recharge of GROUNDWATER.

Several areas of hydrology need additional research. Water resource management and river forecasting are important if the effects of seasonal droughts and floods are to be minimized. Future water resources will have to provide a water supply for an ever-increasing industrial society and population, and proper management is the only answer. Pollution, recreation, and preservation of a suitable environment for fish and wildlife are additional problems that must be solved.

Urban hydrology research has not received the attention needed to provide for a better management of the dwindling water

supplies of metropolitan areas. The need is also great for a better understanding of fresh water lakes and rivers. Continued research into the circulation patterns of the oceans is a necessity if we are to conserve and make better use of our water resources.

P.P.S.

SEE ALSO: OCEANS, WATER CYCLE

International Oceanographic Decade

During the late 1960s the United States recognized the need for, and importance of, continued exploration of the oceans. It established several long-range programs, such as the International Oceanographic Decade, which started in 1970, to gain a better understanding of the marine *habitat.* It began a series of intense investigations to examine different aspects of the oceans: future mining of the sea floor, effects of marine pollution on sea life, and the possibility of underwater communities where people may eventually live and work.

Many problems result from people's exploitation of the oceans. Of these, overuse and continued pollution are of primary concern. The oceans are being used as industrial dumping areas for many types of waste. Many parts of the Baltic, Mediterranean, and Caspian seas are already heavily polluted with globs of oil, tar, and plastics. Marine life in these areas is severely threatened. Overfishing has greatly depleted many rich fishing areas. Steps must be taken to protect the entire marine environment. *The Law of the Sea Conference* is an attempt to establish a means of dealing with pollution problems. Most organizations that promote and coordinate marine-related activities fall within the United Nations system. The UNESCO (United Nations Educational, Scientific, and Cultural Organization) program is concerned with stimulating and coordinating a wide range of oceanic research. Several of the programs have been the International Oceanographic Commission, International Indian Ocean Expedition, and the Cooperative Investigations of the Mediterranean. P.P.S.

SEE ALSO: GLOMAR CHALLENGER, OCEAN, OCEANOGRAPHY.

Basic SI Units		
Physical Quantity	SI Unit	Symbol
length	meter	m
mass	kilogram	kg
time	second	s
electric current	ampere	A
thermodynamic temperature	kelvin	K
amount of substance	mole	mol
luminous intensity	candela	cd
SI units with special names		
Physical Quantity	SI Unit	Symbol
frequency	hertz	Hz
energy	joule	J
force	newton	N
power	watt	W
pressure	pascal	Pa
electric charge	coulomb	C
potential difference	volt	V
resistance	ohm	Ω
capacitance	farad	F
conductance	stemens	S
magnetic flux	weber	Wb
inductance	henry	H
magnetic flux density	telsa	T
luminous flux	lumen	lm
illumination	lux	lx

International System of Units The International System of Units is a variation of the metric system. It was developed by a committee of the INTERNATIONAL BUREAU OF WEIGHTS AND MEASURES. The French name for this system is *Le Systeme International d' Unités*. The French name is abbreviated SI.

The International System of Units defines the basic unit of measure for every physical property. The SI unit can be a basic unit or a combination of basic units. The combinations are called *derived* units.

The system also includes a series of prefixes. Most of the prefixes are in intervals of 1,000 or 1×10^3.

BASIS OF UNITS

There are seven basic units: meter for length; kilogram for mass; second for time; amperes for electric current; kelvin for temperature; mole for the amount of a substance; and candela for light intensity.

The meter (m) is defined as 1,650,763.73 wave lengths in a vacuum of the orange-red line in the spectrum of krypton-86. The SI unit for area is meters squared (m^2). The SI unit for volume is meters cubed (m^3).

The kilogram (kg) is defined in terms of a cylinder of platinum-iridium alloy. This cylinder is located at the International Bureau of Weights and Measures in Sevres, France. A duplicate of this standard is at the National Bureau of Standards in Washington, D.C. This is the only basic unit that is defined in terms of an object.

The unit of force is a newton (N). The newton is a force that, acting on a one-kilogram mass, produces an acceleration of one meter per second per second. The SI unit for work and energy is a joule (J). A joule is a force of one newton acting over a range of one meter. The SI unit of power is a watt (W). The watt is the rate at which work is done or energy is used per second. The SI unit for pressure is a pascal (Pa).

The term degree is not used with the thermodynamic temperature scale. A kelvin (K) is the unit for temperature. The kelvin is defined in terms of the triple point of water. The triple point is the temperature at which ice, water vapor, and liquid water are present at the same time. The kelvin is 1/273.16 the thermodynamic temperature of the triple point of water. Zero kelvin is called ABSOLUTE ZERO, the lowest possible temperature.

The ampere (A) is the basic unit for electric current. The ampere is defined as the current that, if maintained in each of two parallel wires one meter apart in space, will produce a force between the two wires of 2×10^{-7} newtons for each meter of length. The force is due to the magnetic field around the wire. The SI unit for voltage is the VOLT (v). The SI unit for resistance is the OHM (Ω). The SI unit for charge is the COULOMB (C). The SI unit for capacitance is the FARAD (F). The SI unit for conductance is the siemens (S). The SI unit for magnetic flux is the weber (Wb). The SI unit for flux density is the telsa (T). The SI unit for inductance is the henry (H).

The candela (cd) is defined as the lumious intensity of 1/600,000 of a square meter on a black body at a temperature of freezing platinum (2045°K). The unit of light flow is the lumen (lm). A source with an intensity of one candela in all directions radiates a light flux of 4 π lumens.

The mole is defined as the amount of a substance that contains as many particles as there are atoms in .012 kilograms of carbon-12. The particles can be atoms, molecules, ions, electrons, or other particles or groups of particles. The SI unit of concentration is moles per cubic meter.

The second (s) is defined as the duration of 9,192,631,770 absorptions and emissions of radiation of the atoms of cesium-133. The number of events or cycles per second is called frequency. The unit of frequency, a cycle per second, is hertz (Hz). The unit for velocity is meter per second. The unit for acceleration is meters per second per second.

The prefixes used in the International System of Units are:

Whole number multiples			Fractional multiples		
Power of ten	Prefix	Symbol	Power of ten	Prefix	Symbol
10^{12}	tera	T	10^{-1}	deci	d
10^{9}	giga	G	10^{-2}	centi	c
10^{6}	mega	M	10^{-3}	milli	m
10^{3}	kilo	k	10^{-6}	micro	μ
10^{2}	hecto	h	10^{-9}	nano	n
10^{1}	deca	da	10^{-12}	pico	p
			10^{-15}	femto	f
			10^{-18}	atto	a

For example, 1,000 meters or 10^3 meters equals 1 kilometer; one centimeter equals 1/100 or 10^{-2} meters.　　A.J.H.

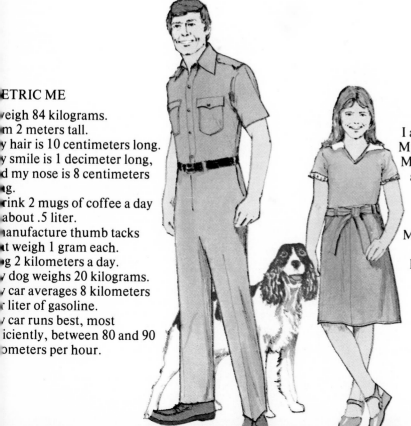

ETRIC ME

eigh 84 kilograms.
m 2 meters tall.
y hair is 10 centimeters long.
y smile is 1 decimeter long,
d my nose is 8 centimeters
g.
rink 2 mugs of coffee a day
about .5 liter.
anufacture thumb tacks
t weigh 1 gram each.
g 2 kilometers a day.
y dog weighs 20 kilograms.
y car averages 8 kilometers
r liter of gasoline.
y car runs best, most
iciently, between 80 and 90
ometers per hour.

METRIC ME

I weigh 30 kilograms.
I am 1 meter 2 decimeters tall.
My hair is 45 centimeters long.
My smile is 8 centimeters long
and my nose is 4 centimeters
long.
I drink 1 liter of milk every
two days.
My favorite tiny pencil weighs
5 grams.
My small fish bowl holds 900
milliliters of water.

Conversion Factors to Metric Measurement

Length
1 inch = 25.4 millimeters (mm) exactly
1 inch = 2.54 centimeters (cm) exactly
1 foot = 0.3048 meters (m) exactly
1 yard = 0.9144 meters (m) exactly
1 mile = 1.609344 kilometers (km) exactly

Area
1 square inch = 6.4516 square centimeters (cm^2) exactly
1 square foot = 0.092903 square meters (m^2)
1 square yard = 0.836127 square meters (m^2)
1 square acre = 0.404686 hectares (ha)
1 square mile = 2.58999 square kilometers (km^2)

Cubic Measure
1 cubic inch = 16.387064 cubic centimeters (cm^3) exactly
1 cubic foot = 0.0283168 cubic meters (m^3)
1 cubic yard = 0.764555 cubic meters (m^3)

US Liquid Measure
1 fluid ounce = 29.5735 milliliters (ml)
1 fluid ounce = 0.2957 deciliters (dl)
1 pint = 0.473176 liters (l)
1 gallon = 3.78541 liters (l)

US Dry Measure
1 pint = 0.550610 liters (l)
1 bushel = 35.2391 liters (l)

Weight
1 grain = 0.0647989 grams (g)
1 ounce = 28.3495 grams (g)
1 pound = 0.453592 kilograms (kg)
1 short ton = 0.907185 metric tons (t)
1 UK ton = 1.01605 metric tons (t)

Temperature
To convert Fahrenheit to Centigrade (Celsius) complete the following
equation. $(F° - 32) \times 5 \div 9 = C°$